LAYMAN'S BIBLE BOOK COMMENTARY

JEREMIAH, LAMENTATIONS

VOLUME 11

Edward R. Dalglish

BROADMAN PRESS
Nashville, Tennessee

4211-81

ISBN: 0-8054-1181-X

Dewey Decimal Classification: 224.2

Subject Headings:
BIBLE. O.T. JEREMIAH / / BIBLE. O.T. LAMENTATIONS.

Library of Congress Catalog Card Number: 81-65801

Printed in the United States of America

The writer would like to acknowledge his indebtedness to his revered and learned teacher, Dean Charles Lincoln Taylor, late professor of Old Testament at Episcopal Theological Seminary in Cambridge, Massachusetts, who first opened up to him the great and abiding riches of the Book of Jeremiah, and to his kindly wife Margaret and the family, who graciously donated the Dean's lecture notes, unpublished manuscripts, and a portion of his fine library to Baylor University. These resources have made the task of writing the commentary more enjoyable. He cannot forget the inspiration of his two helpmeets: one who encouraged him always, Florence Margaret Dalglish, ob. 1974, and Margaret S. Dalglish, who now encourages him.

Foreword

The *Layman's Bible Book Commentary* in twenty-four volumes was planned as a practical exposition of the whole Bible for lay readers and students. It is based on the conviction that the Bible speaks to every generation of believers but needs occasional reinterpretation in the light of changing language and modern experience. Following the guidance of God's Spirit, the believer finds in it the authoritative word for faith and life.

To meet the needs of lay readers, the *Commentary* is written in a popular style, and each Bible book is clearly outlined to reveal its major emphases. Although the writers are competent scholars and reverent interpreters, they have avoided critical problems and the use of original languages except where they were essential for explaining the text. They recognize the variety of literary forms in the Bible, but they have not followed documentary trails or become preoccupied with literary concerns. Their primary purpose was to show what each Bible book meant for its time and what it says to our own generation.

The Revised Standard Version of the Bible is the basic text of the *Commentary*, but writers were free to use other translations to clarify an occasional passage or sharpen its effect. To provide as much interpretation as possible in such concise books, the Bible text was not printed along with the comment.

Of the twenty-four volumes of the *Commentary*, fourteen deal with Old Testament books and ten with those in the New Testament. The volumes range in pages from 140 to 168. Four major books in the Old Testament and five in the New are treated in one volume each. Others appear in various combinations. Although the allotted space varies, each Bible book is treated as a whole to reveal its basic message with some passages getting special attention. Whatever plan of Bible study the reader may follow, this *Commentary* will be a valuable companion.

Despite the best-seller reputation of the Bible, the average survey of Bible knowledge reveals a good deal of ignorance about it and its primary meaning. Many adult church members seem to think that its study is intended for children and preachers. But some of the newer translations have been making the Bible more readable for all ages. Bible study has branched out from Sunday into other days of the week, and into neighborhoods rather than just in churches. This *Commentary* wants to meet the growing need for insight into all that the Bible has to say about God and his world and about Christ and his fellowship.

BROADMAN PRESS

Contents

JEREMIAH

LAMENTATIONS

JEREMIAH

Introduction

The Contemporary Historical Scene

The Book of Jeremiah embraces a period beginning with 627 BC, the date of Jeremiah's calling in the thirteenth year of the Judean king Josiah (640-609 BC) and extends a decade or so after the fall of Jerusalem in 587 BC. The data are supplied in 2 Kings 22—25, 2 Chronicles 34—36, Jeremiah, Lamentations, and such contemporary prophets as Ezekiel, Isaiah (chs. 40—55), Zephaniah, Obadiah, and Nahum.

The boy-king Josiah (640-609 BC) during the period of his youth must have been guided by men of true prophetic vision. They implanted within him the burning desire to reform Judah both politically and religiously. The Chronicler noted that when Josiah was but a youth of sixteen, he set his heart to seek Yahweh. At twenty he began to collect funds in Judah and in the adjacent areas for the repair of the Temple and the rebuilding of Judean power. In his eighteenth year of rule (621 BC), at age twenty-six, a book of the law was found in the renovation of the Temple. It was apparently an abridged version of our present Deuteronomy, perhaps chapters 12—26. This discovery by Hilkiah the high priest was immediately announced to the king by Shaphan, the secretary of state. Alarmed at its ominous threats Josiah sent a delegation bearing the newly-found scroll to Huldah, a nationally-recognized prophetess, and was informed by her that the evils forecast in the scroll were imminent upon the Judean state. Immediately the king instituted a far-reaching reform both religious and moral in character, with political overtones, since the purge of the Temple meant the repudiation of the Assyrian reign.

The radical cleansing of the Temple uncovered the abominations that had been adopted by the wayward kings of Judah. The utensils for the service of Baal, Asherah, and the astral hosts were burned, the idolatrous priests of Baal were removed, the house for the cult prostitutes in the Temple, where women wove hangings for the

Asherah, was destroyed, the divine horses for the sun and the altars situated on the roof of the palace of Ahaz were demolished, and the high places built for the Ashtoreth, the goddess of the Sidonians, for Chemosh, the god of Moab, and for Milcom, the god of the Ammonites were eradicated. The reformation of Josiah extended also into the areas of the defunct Northern Kingdom, now a province of a declining Assyrian Empire.

The political activity of Josiah was possible only because Assyria was experiencing domestic problems at home. The declining years of Assurbanipal (669-626 BC) were troublesome years for Assyria. The great assertive energy that had characterized the earlier months had dissipated. The aged king now applied himself to archaeological research and the preservation of the history of his mighty realm by creating a library and busying his scribes in copying cuneiform tablets. Little did he realize that within two decades of his demise the great Assyrian Empire would be no more.

The devastating blow came from Nabopolassar of Babylon (609-605 BC) and Cyaxares of Media (625-585 BC) who joined forces to overthrow Assyria. With the fall of Nineveh in 612 BC, a remnant of the Assyrian army under Asshuruballit II (612-609 BC) regrouped at Haran for a last desperate stand. The Egyptians, who were bound in a common defensive alliance with Assyria, sought to join forces at Haran in order to forestall the menacing power of Nebuchadnezzar, the son of Nabopolassar, and the Babylonian army. To reach his Assyrian allies, Pharaoh Neco II set out in 609 BC for Haran on the upper Euphrates. This traversing of territory now in the hands of Josiah was considered an act of war, and the reforming king engaged the Egyptians in battle. Josiah was apparently unwilling to surrender what he had gained in terms of national freedom and religious reform from the decadent Assyrian state only to forfeit these to Egypt. However, Josiah was slain at Megiddo by the superior Egyptian army, a very dark day, indeed, in the history of Judah (cp. 2 Kings 23:30; 2 Chron. 35:24 ff.).

The Judeans chose the fourth son of Josiah as the new king, but Jehoahaz, known also as Shallum, reigned only three months when he was rudely removed by Neco, who intended to enjoy the spoils of his victory by nominating his own appointee over the newly acquired Judean territory (2 Kings 23:30-32). Summoning Jehoahaz to his headquarters in the field of Riblah, Neco deposed him and took him away into Egypt where he died (2 Kings 23:22; Jer. 22:

10-12; Ezek. 19:1-4). Then Neco invested Jehoiakim as the new monarch and imposed upon him a heavy tribute of one talent of gold and one hundred talents of silver.

Jehoiakim (609-598 BC) was quite the opposite of his father Josiah; he was cruel, selfish, ruthless, covetous, and apparently pro-Egyptian, for this was to his immediate advantage (Jer. 22:12-19). Immediately upon accession to the throne he paid the war indemnity which the Egyptians had laid upon Judah by taxing his people, while at the same time he overbuilt his palatial mansion and defaulted in its payment. His tough policies silenced the opposition; Uriah ben Shemaiah from Kiriathjearim was extradited from Egypt at his behest and put to death (Jer. 26:20 ff.). He would have made short work of Jeremiah, if he had dared, but the prophet had too much support from the nobility and the people to be liquidated. Besides, he could use Jeremiah to curry favor among the prophetic-minded and purists, a not inconsiderable political asset in an uncertain period (Jer. 36:1 ff.).

The changing fortunes of history were soon to confront Jehoiakim, for in 605 BC Nebuchadnezzar followed up the logical sequel to his stunning victory over the Assyrian-Egyptian armies at Haran in 609 BC by undertaking the control of the entire Palestinian coastal region. The Babylonians met the Egyptians initially at Carchemish in 605 BC (Jer. 46), where they won a decisive victory, pursued their advantage at Haran to win a second resounding encounter, and while the Egyptians were reeling back into their own territory with no thought of further engagement, the Babylonians gathered into their empire the cities and petty states from the Euphrates to the brook of Egypt (2 Kings 24:7). Among the captured cities was the Philistine city of Ashkelon which figures in Jeremiah 47 and in archaeology.

Judah now faced a political crisis: she was a state aligned to the vanquished Egyptian power and was momentarily to be challenged by the conquering Babylonians. Jehoiakim called for a national fast (Jer. 36:9) and no doubt put out feelers for a negotiated settlement. The Babylonians accepted the proffered fidelity of Judah without military force, and Jehoiakim now transferred the national loyalty to the Babylonians. This lasted for three years, when the crafty Jehoiakim revolted, perhaps spurred on by Egyptian promises of assistance. He was seized and transported to Babylon for alleged treason. But like Manasseh before him he was acquitted of the charges and restored to his throne (2 Chron. 36:6). Nebuchadnezzar, being engaged elsewhere, did not immediately react to the new defection save to harass Judah with troops of his provincial allies in the west (2 Kings 24:2 ff.); but in 598 BC he himself joined the campaign against rebellious Judah. The incident that concerned Jeremiah and the Rechabites may be placed in this period of siege when the latter took refuge behind the walls of Jerusalem (35:11).

Whether by natural causes or by court assassins, Jehoiakim died before the Babylonian reprisal could be effected (2 Kings 24:1-8; compare Jer. 22:18 ff.). The problem fell upon his son Jehoiachin (known also as Jeconiah or Coniah) who had the good sense to surrender to Nebuchadnezzar in March, 597 BC, after a brief reign of three months. It was a smart move, one that Jeremiah advocated, and saved Judah from untold needless suffering. As it was, the king and the royal family, the nobles and the military, together with ten thousand captives from the artisan class were transported to Babylon in an endeavor to secure for Nebuchadnezzar his western front in Palestine.

Nebuchadnezzar chose Mattaniah as the new king of Judah. He was another son of Josiah and uncle of Jehoiachin. The Babylonian king changed his name to Zedekiah (2 Kings 24:17). The fact that there were now two living Judean kings presented a subtle dynastic problem. While Zedekiah was king *in fact,* Jehoiachin was regarded by his fellow exiles as the rightful king. The imprisoned king was released about 560 BC, after an imprisonment of some thirty-seven years, by the Babylonian monarch Evil Merodach (Amel Marduk), who accorded him an honored place at his table as befitted his station and provided amply for his needs from the royal treasury.

Zedekiah had no easy task confronting him as he attempted to hold the factions together during his first years only to continue to lose the power of his position to his ambitious nobles. Revolt was in the air and was becoming increasingly contagious. When an insurrection broke out in the army of Nebuchadnezzar in 595-4 BC, it was the signal for the rebellious Palestinian states of Edom, Moab, Ammon, Tyre, and Sidon to contemplate rebellion, in which cause they sent envoys to Jerusalem to encourage the wavering Zedekiah to join the revolt (27:3 ff.). While Judah declined to participate at that time, and was spared the punitive campaign which Nebuchadnezzar launched against the rebels in 594, the pressure of the pro-Egyptian party became more and more difficult to resist, particularly when the new Egyptian pharaohs reversed the policy of Neco II and became actively engaged in stirring revolt against Babylon. Fanatic nationalism precipitated the final rebellion in 589. In the revolt only Tyre and Ammon joined Judah; Edom ultimately aligned herself with the Babylonian cause (Obad. 10-14; Lam. 4:21-22; Ps. 137:7). The following year, in 588 (2 Kings 25:1; Jer. 52:4), Jerusalem was besieged (21:3 ff.), with Judean cities and strongholds being taken as well. Only the powerful fortresses of Lachish and Azekah held out (34:6).

Some months after Jerusalem was surrounded, the Babylonian forces withdrew, a move occasioned by the news that an Egyptian army was advancing to relieve Jerusalem (Jer. 37:5). This state of affairs did not last long, for the Babylonians promptly beat the Egyptians and reestablished the siege of Jerusalem. Month after month until a year had passed, the war-weary defenders of Jerusalem endured the insufferable agonies of a siege: famine, plague, death, and despair (21:7,9; 34:17 ff.). In July, 587, the Babylonians breached the walls and entered the city. Zedekiah, with some of the military, attempted an escape under the cover of darkness, hoping to make it to Ammon, but they were apprehended in the Plains of Jericho (2 Kings 25:3 ff.; Jer. 52:7). Transported to the headquarters of Nebuchadnezzar at Riblah, Zedekiah saw his sons slain before he himself was forcibly blinded and bound over for exile in Babylon where he died (2 Kings 25:6; Jer. 52:9 ff.; compare 34:4 ff.). Several weeks later Nebuzaradan, the commander of the guard of Nebuchadnezzar, took over Jerusalem, burned the city, and leveled its walls. Some of the important persons from the various sectors of society were tried as war criminals before Nebuchadnezzar in Riblah and were summarily executed. Some eight hundred and thirty-two others were rounded up for Exile in Babylon (52:24 ff.). The poorest peasants of the land of Judah were permitted to maintain their residence and to preserve the agriculture of the land (52:16).

With the fall of Jerusalem in 587 BC Nebuchadnezzar incorporated the kingdom of Judah as a province within the Babylonian Empire and set Gedaliah, a prominent Judean, over it as governor (Jer. 40:5,7-12; 2 Kings 25:22-24). The new governor was of noble lineage and had served as one of the chief ministers in the court of Zedekiah. Confident of his people and of his program, he sought to establish a peaceful return to some degree of normalcy through enlightened cooperation with Babylon. Taking up his residence in Mizpah he refused to be dissuaded from his purposes by rumors of an assassination plot (40:13 ff.), nor would he ferret out the alleged conspirators. His confidence cost him his life, for Ishmael, a member of the royal house, with a party of ten men murdered the new governor, his immediate associates, and members of the Babylonian garrison stationed at Mizpah.

The fearful state of affairs that had now developed in the Babylonian province of Judah, with Nebuchadnezzar's nominee brutally murdered by a disgruntled member of the king's family, was an explosive situation. The people of consequence rallied about Johanan, the son of Kareah, and Azariah, the son of Hoshaiah, both involved in the military. Despite their appeal to Jeremiah, who counseled them to abide in Judah and to discount any serious reprisals from Babylon, the leaders and the people panicked and made their way to Egypt, taking Jeremiah along, since he had won the confidence of the Babylonians and might cushion whatever shock might be forthcoming from Mesopotamia (chs. 42—44).

A few personal incidents in the life of Jeremiah, which will be discussed next, and information drawn from other sources such as Lamentations, Ezekiel, and Isaiah (40—66) present a somber picture of the Judeans during the next half century. The Exile had been predicted to last some seventy years (25:11 f.), a period long and difficult, but a period of spiritual awakening and moral advance. The Judeans realized then the unique ministry of Jeremiah, the truth of his proclamation, and consoled themselves in the hope of restoration which he had forecasted (29:10).

The Personal Life of Jeremiah

Jeremiah was born in Anathoth, a village in the land assigned to the tribe of Benjamin, which may be identified with the modern Ras Kharrubeh, located some two miles northeast of Jerusalem. Jeremiah was the son of Hilkiah and was descended from the honorable but deposed priesthood of the family of Abiathar. It is possible to draw some inferences from his family background.

First, Jeremiah identified himself with the tribal tradition of Benjamin, even though he was a Levite, and was keenly aware of the royal role the tribe of Benjamin had played. Not far from his home was the sepulcher of Rachel, the mother of Benjamin. The moving reference to Rachel as weeping for the tragedy of the contemporary hour suggests how deeply Jeremiah was attached to the northern traditions (31:15). Early in his ministry he addressed two sermons to Northern Israel (actually an Assyrian province but now without effective tributary bonds as Assyria rapidly declined) to return to the better ways of Yahwism (2:4 to 3:5; 3:6-22). Moreoever, he clearly associated the former Northern Kingdom of Israel with Judah in the future restoration and union of the Israelite nation.

Second, that Jeremiah was born in a village under the cultural influence of Jerusalem is evidenced clearly in his life and experience. Jerusalem was the capital of Judah, the locale of the royal house of David, and the site of the religious center of the nation. Its cosmopolitanism, culture, closeness to the cutting edge of domestic and international politics, and religious significance probably greatly influenced the smart and impressionable youth. More and more he gravitated to Jerusalem until he permanently went to live there.

Third, the experience of being an eyewitness to the daily happenings in the capital was invaluable as a preparation for his incisive analysis and penetrating judgment of the affairs of state.

Fourth, the accessibility of Jerusalem with its cosmopolitanism and culture appears to have made its impression on Jeremiah. Scribal schools with a curriculum of reading, writing, literature, history, and moral philosophy or studies in the wisdom heritage must have flourished in the capital. The overtones of moral philosophy are clearly seen in the prophets of Israel. The optimistic, the defense of God's goodness, and the pessimistic, such as are discovered in the Books of Proverbs, Job, and Ecclesiastes respectively, find their counterpart in the thought of the prophets (Amos, Habakkuk, Haggai, Jeremiah). Jeremiah betrays this influence in his use of popular proverbs (31:29), moral precepts (9:22), wisdom sayings (17:5-8), and religious principles (10:23; 17:9).

And, finally, the early training and later experience of Jeremiah caused him to become a serious student of his nation's history and a good analyst of the political, social, and religious problems of his day. His writings betray the profound indebtedness he owed to his intellectual teachers. Sixty-six passages in Deuteronomy are quoted not less than eighty-six places in his book. Hosea, the northern prophet of the eighth century to Israel and akin to Jeremiah in extraction, temperament, and religious convictions, profoundly affected Jeremiah, as may be gathered from some twenty passages Jeremiah uses from that book. The prophet of Anathoth was deeply read in Israelite history. He had a wide experience and an excellent education to formulate the manifesto for the benefit of his nation—even the consultations of the kings with the prophet supports such a thesis.

The personality of Jeremiah has been variously viewed. Some make it out to be very sensitive, shy, introspective, individualistic rather than social, timid rather than courageous, and fearful rather than brave. Such a characterization is largely drawn from a misinterpretation of Jeremiah, chapter 1, where he objected to his call to be a prophet, alleging that he was but a "youth" and where Yahweh urged him to banish his fear (vv. 6 ff.). Additional data for such a concept has been drawn from his introspective "confessions." But such a view is decidedly exaggerated. His objection and his fear in the call experience betray no weakness or fearful desire to escape. They represent rather an honest and courageous appraisal of his felt inadequacy in view of the overwhelming challenge of the mission. There is no shade of timidity or retirement before opposition anywhere in his experience. Sensitive he might be, but never a coward; fearless in the face of opposition, willing to endure injustice for his outspokenness, but never retraction and giving in. Jeremiah had strength of character and that against a national majority.

Jeremiah has also been described as "one against the world." It is only too true that he felt abysmally lonely on occasion (15:17). He longed for the comfort and companionship of wife and family but would not involve them in his difficulties (16:1). At times he was depressed (15:10; 20:14-18) and felt keenly the rejection of his people (9:1 ff.). In his call he had been frankly warned that his mission would antagonize the king and his nobles, the prophets and the priests, and the unthinking people. His greatest fear was neither death nor the combat of unrighteousness and apostasy nor exposing the religious hypocrisy and the devastating policies of state. His greatest fear was that he might lose Yahweh somewhere in the darkness, somewhere in the insoluble problems that vexed his days. Admittedly, it was a very hard lot, but it was softened by the supportive fellowship of God. His lot was tempered by having such a loyal secretary as Baruch, a fact that indicates that Jeremiah was not without trustworthy friends among the servants of the king and the nobles.

It has generally been assumed that the initial stages of the ministry of Jeremiah were concerned with the propagation of the book of the law found in the Temple in 621 BC. Thus radical reform is thought to be the thesis of his preaching throughout the cities of Judah. It is further assumed that the response of the Judeans was decidedly superficial and that Jeremiah repudiated the legalistic approach as insufficient to change the ethical structure of the nation. The rejection of this early ministry is allegedly implicit in 8:8. "How can you say, 'We are wise,/and the law of the Lord is with us'?/But, behold, the false pen of the scribes/has made it into a lie."

Postulating such an early ministry for Jeremiah is very speculative. It is wiser to draw broader patterns of his early days from his writings. It seems clear that the prophet began at Anathoth and, being rejected there, moved on to Jerusalem. Probably any reform would have been welcomed by Jeremiah, particularly that in which Josiah engaged (2 Kings 23), for whom he had high praise (11:15 ff.). The book found in the Temple had a profound influence on Jeremiah. Moreover, when Josiah was slain, the Chronicler recorded how tragic the loss was for Jeremiah (2 Chron. 35:25). In place of an assumed period of silent withdrawal, one may better substitute a picture of Jeremiah cooperating in every way with the reforming king. Jeremiah 1—6 stresses the moral demands of Yahweh, the need for amendment of life, and other Deuteronomic themes. Since this block of material is generally dated in the days of Josiah, it would seem to reflect overtones of Deuteronomy and aspects of the reformation of Josiah.

The preaching of Jeremiah during the days of Josiah (chs. 1—6) displays the finesse of his poetry: its sensitiveness, its roving range, its changing images, its lyric depths, and its fresh and moving vigor. Jeremiah is not attempting to be a great poet; he is attempting to effect moral improvement in the nation. The passion for his task becomes the passion of his poetry. No other prophet was so keenly sensitive to the past, for the great days of yore; none was more bewildered at the present deterioration. Question follows question, argument heaps upon argument, plea joins to plea to stress the divine solicitude and the perverse response of the nation. Jeremiah denounced political and religious parties motivated by self-interest, rampant idolatrous practices, monstrous customs and unethical conduct that was followed with an incredible profession of innocence. Judgment hastens; the nation is ripe. A foe from the north, best considered a foreign enemy, will be the rod of Yahweh's chastisement (1:13 ff.; 4:5-31; 5:15-17; 6:22-27, etc.).

Jeremiah was profoundly interested in the devastated land to the north, the former kingdom of Israel, and addressed the survivors there to amend their ways and build their future in fellowship with Yahweh (3:12 to 4:4). It seems evident that Jeremiah espoused the hope that a moral Judah and Israel could be reunited and pursue the messianic role and goal of the elect nation (4:17 ff.). The success that Josiah achieved in his reformation and in the enlargement of his kingdom must have created hopes in the heart of the faithful that the messianic times, the fulfillment of the Davidic promises, were to be realized. The preaching of Jeremiah during the days of Josiah had an optimistic ring that was lost after the tragic death of the king.

The ministry of Jeremiah during the days of Jehoiakim met with opposition almost at every turn. Judah was subjugated by the Egyptians after the death of Josiah in 609 BC and then fell under the domination of the Babylonians in 605 BC. The dream of liberation was over; new plans had to be drawn; new personnel thwarted the prophetic goals.

Jeremiah witnessed the vain attempt of Judah to crown Jehoahaz (or Shallum) as the successor to Josiah. He bid his countrymen weep for the quickly deposed monarch, for as a captive he would be hauled into Egypt never to return (22:10-12; compare Ezek. 19:1-4). In the assertion of Palestinian sovereignty the Egyptian pharaoh placed Jehoiakim upon the throne in 609; and for eleven years Judah was harassed by Egypt and then Babylon, by oppressive policies of the king at home, and by serious divisions within the nation itself.

Jeremiah's relationship to Jehoiakim was extremely distant and strained. The monarch viewed the free church prophets with a guarded hatred. On one occasion he was so infuriated that the prophet Uriah was preaching a doctrine similar to Jeremiah's that he killed him (26:20 ff.). The forthright message of Jeremiah served to anger the king immensely, as the so-called Temple sermon evidences (Jer. 7 and 26). The bold plea of the prophet for the correction of the national life was indirectly a repudiation of the policies of state and of church. Jeremiah protested the vain assurance of the royal priests, who insisted that Jerusalem and its Temple could never be taken (7:4,10 ff.). Instead, Jeremiah advocated a renewed allegiance to moral standards of justice, honesty, purity, and fidelity which alone would guarantee the future. Relentlessly, the prophet exposed the idolatrous vanities of the nation (7:16 ff.), the ineffectiveness of the sacrificial practices, and the immoral behavior of the nation. He forecasted that it would end in disaster and cited the destruction of the tabernacle at Shiloh as an example. Such a blistering attack upon the religious life and the unethical beliefs of the citizenry, delivered within the precincts of the Temple by a radical reforming prophet, caused Jeremiah to be seized by the priests and other prophets and hastened to trial for his alleged blasphemies. Only the skillful pleading of some friendly nobles, who cited the earlier case of the prophet Micah, secured the release of the prophet (ch. 26).

The year 605 BC was a memorable one: it was the first year of Nebuchadnezzar and the fourth year of Jehoiakim of Judah. Three events share the importance: (1) Nebuchadnezzar soundly defeated the Egyptian Neco II at Carchemish, and Judah became a province of Babylon. Jeremiah saluted the conqueror with a stirring military poem (ch. 46), for the Babylonian rule through the Fertile Crescent was seen by the prophet as consistent with the purposes of Yahweh. (2) The blueprint of Jeremiah outlined the future: the past twenty-three years of his ministry had met with stout resistance; judgment from Yahweh would assume the form of an exile of seventy years; and thereafter Babylon herself would be judged (ch. 25). (3) Jeremiah was inwardly moved to gather all the words which he had uttered against Judah and the nations and write them in a scroll. Once the scroll was completed, Baruch read the document to the Judean worshipers on a fast day in the Temple. It was a serious indictment of an ungrateful nation. The contents of the scroll were immediately communicated to the nobles at the palace; they deemed the matter so serious that it was brought before the king. Bidding Jeremiah and Baruch to hide themselves, they read the scroll to Jehoiakim. As it was read, he cut off column after column and cast it into the brazier that burned before him. He ordered Jeremiah and Baruch to be apprehended, but Jeremiah and Baruch were well hidden (ch. 36).

Jeremiah was then urged to rewrite the scroll containing all the words he had uttered during the twenty-three years of his ministry in his criticism of Judah and the nations. This he did and added other materials to the new scroll. One may conjecture that the so-called Confessions (11:18-23; 12:1-6; 15:10 ff.,15-21; 17:14-18; 18:18-23; 20:7-18) were added and that the completed scroll contained much of the material now present in chapters 1—25. The actual experiences of Jeremiah during the last years of Jehoiakim are not described in detail, but as the perceptive moral critic of the nation

Jeremiah must have had deep moments of despair as the crises deepened.

Retribution came in March 597 when Nebuchadnezzar succeeded in capturing Jerusalem. Jeremiah had opposed the rebellion and censured the crown for the repudiation of its oath (27:6 ff.). Whether Jehoiakim died naturally or was assassinated by intrigue remains unknown, but Jeremiah did predict that his death would occasion no sorrow and his funeral would resemble that of an unclean ass (22:18-23)!

Nebuchadnezzar deposed Jehoiachin the successor of Jehoiakim after a reign of three months. Some ten thousand Judeans were exiled to Babylon, most of whom were of the upper social register, including the king and his court. Jeremiah composed an oracle on the occasion of the exile of the Judean king in which he affirmed that Jehoiachin would never return to his native land and that his seed would have no further participation in the Davidic throne (22:24-30).

The political situation for Judah was now complicated by the fact that there were two kings: Zedekiah, the king in fact and Jehoiachin, the king by right in exile. Moreover, the very influential group of exiled Judeans exerted considerable influence on the remnant in Judah. *Meddlesomeness* might be a better term. There arose a tension between those in Judah and those in Babylon. The exiles viewed the Judeans as incompetent and sought to impose their policies upon them. The Judeans regarded the exiles as the filthy rich, the upper crust, who were now justly atoning for their past guilt. Jeremiah made a courageous decision when he related his vision of the two baskets of figs, identifying the basket of good figs as the exiles, the other of rotten figs as the Judeans (ch. 24). The basis for the prophet's judgment may be gathered from the enormities, recited by Ezekiel, which were practiced in Jerusalem (Ezek. 22).

There are a number of oracles and experiences of Jeremiah which may be dated in the beginning of the reign of Zedekiah. To this period is assigned 49:34-39, an oracle against Elam, and a scroll which Jeremiah authored and sent with Seraiah the quartermaster destined to the Babylonian exiles in the fourth year of Zedekiah. The subject of the scroll had as its burden the oracles written concerning the ultimate fall of Babylon (51:59-64). Jeremiah sent another letter to the Babylonian exiles admonishing them to plan for a stay of some seventy years and to resist the vain hopes of the misguided prophets in their midst who were predicting a speedy return to the homeland (29:1-20).

At some time during 594 envoys from Edom, Moab, Ammon, Tyre, and Sidon arrived in Jerusalem with stealthy plans to involve Judah in a concerted rebellion against Babylonian authority in Palestine. Jeremiah dramatically opposed the conference and indicated to the various participants that the God of Israel had given his servant Nebuchadnezzar the land he now occupied and that any course of action other than submission would be fraught with disaster despite the support of the prophets and diviners who were one in their encouragement of the revolt (ch. 27).

A second delegation was sent to Jeremiah by Zedekiah during the dark days of the siege. It was headed by Pashhur and Zephaniah to inquire of Yahweh concerning the outcome of the desperate situation and to implore for some miraculous intervention to save the nation. Jeremiah replied that the Babylonians would be victorious despite all Judean efforts and that the counsel of wisdom was an immediate surrender to the foe. Moreover, the prophet advised the royal house to institute while it might a moral reformation and to divest itself of its vain and complacent optimism (ch. 21).

In the final months of the siege Zedekiah had endured all he could of the threatening of doom by Jeremiah. The prophet had consistently maintained that Jerusalem was to fall into the hands of the Babylonians and that the only sensible thing to do was to surrender. Such forecasts were weakening the morale of the Judeans. Accordingly, the king shut up Jeremiah in the court of the guard which was in the palace of the king (32:1-5).

As the military situation worsened in Jerusalem, with food supplies exhausted, with disease rampant, with the spirit of the defenders lost, and deserters multiplying daily, the leaders were in no mood to tolerate discordant voices. When the chief nobles heard repeatedly that Jeremiah was openly advocating surrender, a group waited on the king and demanded the death penalty for Jeremiah's treasonable words. They pointed out that he was breaking the spirit of the soldiers and the people and had no real interest in the welfare of the nation. The threatened Zedekiah delivered the prophet into their hands. They promptly put him into the cistern of Malchiah in the court of the guard which, fortunately, was without water at the time (38:1-6). However, the mud in the bottom of the cistern spelled

illness and death in its dank depth. Jeremiah was mercifully rescued
by a servant of the king, Ebed-melech, who drew Jeremiah from the
cistern and returned him to the court of the guard (38:7-13). It was
the kindness of a stranger, for Ebed-melech was an Ethiopian! This
singular act of mercy was made the subject of a consoling oracle
which Jeremiah presented to Ebed-melech, assuring him that in the
fall of the city his life would be saved (39:15-18).

When the Babylonians took Jerusalem, they treated the prophet
with great respect and consideration. In a way he had been pro-
Babylonian in that he protested the rebellion and the false faith.
Then in the war between Judah and Babylon he had urged
surrender in the most unequivocal terms. This accounts, no doubt,
for his kindly fate when the city fell. Apparently, Jeremiah was taken
to the headquarters of the Babylonians at Rizpah together with
many Judean captives. There he was given the option to go into
Babylon with the exiles and be assured of excellent provisions (40:4)
or to join the party of Nebuchadnezzar's nominee Gedaliah at
Mizpah. Or, if neither pleased him, he could do what he wished—
he was a free man. Jeremiah chose to go to Mizpah and to be
associated with the survivors remaining in Judah.

The newly-installed governor Gedaliah was ruthlessly assassinated by the witless Ishmael, who multiplied his sins at Mizpah by
unprovoked and senseless slaughter, then made off to Ammon (ch.
41). The Judeans who were left at Mizpah and in Judah were rightly
concerned with what might be ruthless reprisals by the Babylonians
for the murders perpetrated by Ishmael. Under the leadership of
Johanan and Azariah the people determined to flee for safety into
Egypt, but before doing so, sought an oracle of Yahweh from
Jeremiah as to the advisability of such a procedure. After a period of
ten days, Jeremiah ascertained that the people should remain in the
land of Judah and should discount the fear of retaliation. This
advice, however, did not satisfy them; in fact, they suggested that
Jeremiah was lying and that Baruch had suggested what he had
proposed. Accordingly, they took Jeremiah and Baruch into Egypt,
into the city of Tahpanhes. There Jeremiah enacted a mime by
taking large stones and hiding them in the mortar of the pavement at
the entrance of the palace of Pharaoh and then prophesied that upon
these very stones Nebuchadnezzar, the king whom they feared,
would spread his royal canopy when he conquered Egypt. The flight

into Egypt would accordingly be no protection from the Babylonian retaliation.

The last days of Jeremiah must have been filled with painful nostalgia as he beheld the Judean emigrants continuing in their idolatrous worship of the queen of heaven. When Jeremiah criticized their alien practices, they stoutly maintained that they intended to persist in them. They argued that all had been well in Judah until that radical Josiah eradicated the worship of their goddess, the queen of heaven. The divinity was thus slighted and, in her anger, brought upon Judah all the calamities that followed. Now, they continued, they were going to reestablish those rites that they had left off so that once again she would smile on their ways and restore them to their native land. It was a repudiation of Yahwism, pure and simple, the renunciation of the reformation of Josiah, and the complete rejection of Jeremiah!

The death of Jeremiah is not recorded. Tradition suggests that he was stoned to death by his fellow Judeans. There must have been deep sorrow in the heart of the aged prophet when he thought of what could have been but which now was forever forfeited. And yet he was the prophet of the restoration, the herald of the coming days, the seer who saw beyond the immediate devastation to the glorious fulfillment of Israel in history. Those hopes must have consoled him though their light would not dawn upon him. However dark, then, the present and how insuperable the problems, Jeremiah must have been to the end "a defenced city, and an iron pillar, and brasen walls" (1:18, KJV).

Composition of the Book of Jeremiah

Many students of the Bible have found the Book of Jeremiah somewhat difficult to understand. It would be foolish to deny the formidable difficulties in attempting to master the book. The problems arise when we attempt to read into the literature those principles of composition which have been dictated by Western culture. First, the reader should know that the Book of Jeremiah is not chronologically arranged. To illustrate, chapter 24 is assigned to the times of Zedekiah; chapters 25 and 26 to the era of Jehoiakim; chapters 32—34 and 37—38 are placed in the reign of Zedekiah, but chapters 35—36 are ascribed to the times of Jehoiakim.

The reader is also helped by remembering that in poetry and

prose Jeremiah's book has a large variety of literary parts: the sermon (7:1-15), the vision (1:11-14), the invective (8:4-9), the court-room motif (2:5b-12), the apology (defense, 26:12b-15), the proverb (31:29; 17:11; 10:23), the legal discussion (3:1 ff.), the letter (29:1 ff., 24 ff.), the liturgy (14:1 to 15:4), irony (8:7; 22:13; 4:30 ff.), the lament both communal (9:17 ff.) and individual (4:19-22), the unsurpassed lyrical confessions (11:18-23; 12:1-6; 15:10-21; 17:14-18; 18:18-23; 20:7-18), the oracle (21:4-14; 7:16-20), a wisdom psalm (17:5-11), the narrative (chs. 26—29), autobiography (1:4-10), and the military summons (6:1 ff.). This list could be extended, but it will suffice to illustrate the variety of types of literature that are in the Book of Jeremiah.

In the next place, there are superscriptions attached to a number of chapters in the Book of Jeremiah. These headings indicate the time of the composition or, at least, the relevant time of the subject. Included are two from the time of Josiah (1:1-3; 3:6), five from the time of Jehoiakim (25, 26, 35, 36, 45), and thirteen from the time of Zedekiah or later (21, 24, 27, 28, 29, 32, 33, 34, 37, 38, 50, 51, 52). The mixture of compositions from different historical periods is thus easily seen. While there has been some skepticism about the superscriptions which were hardly a part of the original documents, the internal evidence at times fully substantiates the truthfulness of the superscription.

The task of assigning the various parts of Jeremiah to particular occasions and dates is made considerably harder by a number of peculiarities in the book itself. A large amount of the Hebrew text is omitted in the Greek version (100 BC at the latest). Some twenty-seven hundred words or one seventh of the book (something like six or seven chapters all told), have been left out of the Greek version. Moreover, there are numerous repetitions in the Book of Jeremiah itself; these total more than sixty verses (compare, for example, 5:9 with 9:9; 6:22-24 with 50:41-43; 7:16 with 11:14). And, finally, the chapter and verse assignment is a mixed blessing as it presently stands. It was not until the twelfth century AD that the Bible was divided into chapters. It was apparently the work of one man, helpful for the most part, but regrettable on occasion. The division of chapters into verses appears first in the Geneva Bible of 1560. Both chapter and verse divisions impose an interpretative norm, colored with Western culture and imposed upon an ancient Hebrew book. Modern readers are misled quite often by the arbitrariness of the divisions. To illustrate, one may point out that 8:1-3 is the logical ending of chapter 7 and should have been included in chapter 7.

Some readers note Jeremiah's doleful tone with dismay. But the prophet cannot be faulted for the character of his message. Jeremiah had to bear this cross if he would be relevant to his mission and to his day. To be negative, to be rejected for one's words, to lament that all is not well without and within was the badge of his greatness, for only by identification with the sufferings of his people could he gain their ear for the hope and dream after the disaster. Again and again, it is true, Jeremiah returns to his themes: doom, woe, and destruction, the foe from the north, the national illness, the corruption of laity and ruler, and judgment imminent and divine. It needed to be said; he had to say it. If he placed on occasion the poetic laurel on the altar, it was of no account. He was not interested in being a poet, but a man of God with a word for his people.

The Theological Thought of Jeremiah

Theology.—The religious culture in which Jeremiah was nurtured is clearly reflected in the theological affirmations of his writings. The prophets of the eighth century, Amos, Hosea, Isaiah, and Micah, believed that Yahweh, the God of Israel, was equivalent to that ultimate being we call God, that he was almighty, all-wise, and everywhere. From the earliest Mosaic traditions it was affirmed that Yahweh was transcendent over time and space, that he was the sole deity, without a family of sons and daughters (gods and goddesses), and that he was incapable of representation (no idols). Jeremiah espoused this theology as unassailable. Jeremiah worked hard against all such heathen gods which were nonentities and against false ideas about Yahweh born of misconceptions. Yahweh alone was God and as such was the Creator of the world and the director of its destiny. With the unity of God there follows the unity of creation and of purposeful oneness in history.

The entire earth belonged to Yahweh. He was free to do as he willed, and yet in his self-disclosure his will was specified in divine and moral parts so as to rule out all arbitrariness in his governance. Since Yahweh created the world, it has meaning. That meaning was not in the physical universe alone but in humanity, its definitive climax. Here Jeremiah assumed the magnificent views expressed in Hebrew thought, that man was made in the image of God (compare "God . . . breathed into his nostrils the breath of life," Gen. 2:7), that he was an overseer of God over the created world, lacking little of God, and crowned as king with glory and honor (Ps. 8). With man as the object of creation, with man must be the goal of history.

Jeremiah was a prophet to the nations, not merely to Judah. His purpose was to reestablish the spiritually concerned in Judah/Israel to become that messianic people in whom the world would bless itself (4:2). The task of reviving the Judeans so as to assume a national profile would do little in the universal purpose of Yahweh were not that goal the salvation of the nations (Isa. 49:6). The nationalism, militarism, materialism, and isolation of purpose that characterized Israel's history effectively divorced the once Chosen People from the program of Yahweh and rendered the possibilities of fulfilling its spiritual mission in the world as questionable. Jeremiah saw clearly that the nation was unfit for the service of Yahweh, that it would take a cleansing of God to effect a radical change, an experience ultimately provided in the two exiles. Then the nation would be committed to the spiritual values of Yahwism, to evangelism among the nations, and to the enrichment of the entire family of humanity by converting them from the pagan enslavement to the liberation of the emancipating Yahwistic faith.

These overarching theological affirmations generated historical and ethical goals for the Judeans and provided the reason for the prophetic ministry of Jeremiah. If he were not programmed as Isaiah (40—66) in his depiction of Israel as the Suffering Servant engaged in effecting universal salvation, it was because Jeremiah was committed more particularly to the religious and ethical improvement of his people which was a prior condition to their evangelizing the world. To his own nation he dedicated his energies and was committed to that one purpose and to that one purpose alone, to which he freely gave his massive talents and devotion. Such a purpose indicates the thrust of his ministry: its proper subject is man, both in his many ways of defection from God and in his potential perfectability. This is the reason why Jeremiah is the most psychological of all the prophets, the one who most completely analyzed the inner motivations of man and the strange seductions that deceive him.

Anthropology.—Jeremiah began his analysis from the external and progressed toward the inner core. In the first place, the waywardness of Israel was irrational. Beasts act as beasts, birds as birds, but Israel does not function appropriately to the human endowment. Sin did not occur occasionally but was persistently practiced. If a leopard can change his spots or the Ethiopian the color of his skin—two impossible transformations—then, declared Jeremiah, the Judeans who practice evil may do good. The diction of the prophet concerning the sinfulness of Israel is very extensive: dishonesty, oppression, sensuality, apostasy, hardness of feelings, hardness of heart, hard to manage, and so the list goes on. The heart (mind) is stubborn, rebellious, faint, evil, deceitful, corrupt, and so on. Indeed, one of the classic utterances of Jeremiah is to the effect that: "The heart is deceitful above all things,/and desperately corrupt;/who can understand it?" (17:9). This is not applied merely to the moral degenerate, but to all people and to the prophet's own inner life. It embraces such ideas as self-deception, self-pity, self-interest, self-identification, and self-analysis and suggests the possibility for severe margins of error. Jeremiah conceived sin to be inward, ingrained, and demonic. Indeed, it was that inexplicable something beyond the sum total of the components. It was the mystery, the tragedy of a siren voice able to seduce despite every rational attempt to turn from moral suicide.

The prophet saw his contemporaries attempt to escape from the supernatural by plunging into idolatry (10:12-15). This procedure was both rebellious and senseless, and embracing the near, the sensuous, and the material, sometimes by the elevation of sacrifice, circumcision, the law (compare 31:31 ff.), the Temple, or the ark, as a substitute for the true and living God.

Moreover, there is involved an ethical paradox that torments the seeking soul. There are times when sin appears to be a matter of no concern to God (12:1-2).

Jeremiah raises the contradiction of a universe governed by an almighty and righteous God where moral inconsistencies are everywhere apparent. Jeremiah with his "honest to God" attitude articulated this perplexity, for if Jeremiah was totally allied with righteousness, ought not *God* to declare himself openly and everywhere the defender of morality? In the experience of life it is not so seen. The prophet developed his inward hurt about the inequity that he personally endured in his call and mission.

There were occasions when self-pity got to Jeremiah, when he abandoned his post, when he had had enough (15:10 ff.). But in his resignation, he imagined a greater fulfillment. He discovered an identity with the word of Yahweh that was in his soul as a burning

fire and realized that despite its uncertainty, there was no greater
fulfillment than to abide in the center of the will of God. There was
no alternative but to return, to confess his immature attitude, and to
reassume the honor of being a prophet of Yahweh.

*The Confessions of Jeremiah (11:19 to 12:6; 15:10-21; 17:9-18;
18:1-23; 20:7-18).*—These compositions identify with many of the
individual psalms of lamentation rather than with the poetry of the
prophets. In these purely lyrical passages he vented his soul of his
anguish, his doubts, his fears, his resentments over the inequalities
of life, the apparent triumph of evil over good, and the lack of results
of his cross-bearing ministry. On occasion he asked God to visit
wrath upon the wicked (11:20*b*; 12:3*b*; 15:15; 18:21-23; 20:11 ff.) or
pleaded that his innocent suffering for Yahweh's sake be set right
speedily.

But the Confessions are not entirely negative. In the struggle
certain essential truths emerged. The basis of personal religion must
reside in a firm trust in the unerring righteousness of God, despite
all appearances to the contrary. In Jeremiah's desperate plight he
clung to God and committed to him his cause (11:20). The prophet
discovered himself in the crucible of the encounter, an experience
which served as an analysis for his inner motivations. He saw clearly
that to be victorious over others, he had to gain the victory over
himself, to master self-pity, as he fought it out with himself in the
presence of God. This wrestling with God in prayer is the index of
the life of the spirit, and where this type of prayer ceases, spiritual
life dies.

Moreover, the strife showed the importance of being sincere,
"honest to God," whose knowledge of the individual was complete.
Fellowship with God demanded an openhearted sincerity, abandonment of self in the presence of God, and a deep inner self-criticism.
Any self-deception imperiled the health of any meaningful relationship to God or to his service and had to be overcome with its
disillusions.

Jeremiah's struggle did not take place in solitude but in the storm
of persecution and in his own honest and sincere effort to do the will
of God. Success in externalities did not constitute divine approval; it
was rather the establishment of the worth of the individual as he was
driven back to God. It was not the externalities that constituted the
identity of man's worth to God, but the response thereto.

The future and messianic expectations.—The term *messianic* is used in the broadest sense, involving all that pertains to the speaking of the mission of Israel to the world. Unfortunately, much of the experience of Israel was divorced from the goal and destiny inherent in the nation's call (compare Gen. 12:1 ff.; Ex. 19:5 ff.).

Jeremiah had the unenviable task of preparing his nation for the disaster of 586 BC and the three exiles that attended the Judean conquest by the Babylonians. In his inaugural vision (about 627 BC) he was persuaded that "the foe from the north" would one day overrun the land of Judah, with disastrous results. To be sure, now and then he held out the promise of a continuance of the nation in its land if a change of life were immediately forthcoming; but as the years dragged on with deeper and deeper infection invading the national life, the prophet became convinced that the nation must fall. Its political, economic, and social stability had been vastly eroded by the undermining of corruptive religious and ethical practices. In the pluralism of their idolatry there was no one ground of being necessary to maintain national unity, no meaningful ideals to live by and to die for, nothing but selfish confusion compounded. The first twenty-nine chapters of his book are largely devoted to the task of preparing the nation for its fall and exile.

The second task of Jeremiah was to assure his people, that is, those who respected his message, that though they must necessarily be involved in an exile, their continued existence as a messianic people was assured (4:27; 16:14 ff.; 23:3,7 ff.). While this was some softening of the stern announcement of the Exile, it cut off effectively any hope of the exiles ever to return personally to their homeland. The prophet had indicated that the Exile's duration would be some seventy years, so that the hope of a return from exile was actually for the second generation.

A third aspect of Jeremiah's religious forecast was the reunion of the Northern and Southern Kingdoms of Judah. Quite early in his ministry the prophet had proclaimed that the Northern Kingdom was less guilty than Judah and had encouraged Israel to hope for restoration following a genuine change of life (3:6-14). However, the message to Israel and to Judah was one also of sincere repentance. They would find their fulfillment and restoration, both in exile and in homeland, only if Yahwism were the dominating power in their lives. For them to return to Palestine in the same moral status which characterized them before they were exiled would be to effect in no way the great plans of Yahweh for them (29:10 ff.). Here Jeremiah introduced the monumental thought of the New Covenant to come in which there would be a moral inwardness, a fellowship, an unmediated knowledge of Yahweh available to all the faithful and an abundant pardon (31:31 ff.). In one sense it was not new. It had been the experience of the people of God from Abraham onward. It was described in fairly all of its particulars by Isaiah (40—66) and by Ezekiel, both of whom saw the returning exiles as a regenerated, moral, and truly messianic people.

When the people were once again in the Land of Promise, regenerated and united as one people, there would be reestablished the Davidic line of kings—yet with this tremendous difference, they would be knowledgeable shepherds who with wisdom and equity would rule over the restored people. Such leadership would prevent any further enslavement (30:8 ff.) and bring prosperity once again to Israel in terms of national security and material gains, with Temple and palace restored, and the nation enjoying a dynastic regime whose motto would be "[Yahweh] is our righteousness" (23:6; 33:16).

All this is only the preparation for Israel to realize her mission to the world. The cleansing of the Exile would prepare a spiritual people who would be relevant to the entire world. If God can work his purposes through his servant Nebuchadnezzar for Israel (29:9; 27:6; 43:10), he can likewise work out his purposes through Israel to the nations. And if Jeremiah was to be a prophet to the nations to pluck up, to break down, to destroy, and to overthrow (compare 25:30 ff.) he was also to be for them a prophet to build and to plant (1:10; 18:8 ff.).

The truly messianic prophecies in Jeremiah are few in number and limited in scope. They are of great importance nonetheless. When the regenerated Israel is restored to its homeland, "Jerusalem shall be called the throne of [Yahweh], and all nations shall gather to it, to the presence of [Yahweh] in Jerusalem [compare Isa. 2:4], and they shall no more stubbornly follow their own evil heart" (3:17 f.). This may be interpreted to mean that, in the religious and ethical restoration of Israel, the nations will be attracted by its religion and its ethics to become identified with Yahweh, the God of Israel. Jeremiah does not enlarge upon the evangelical mission of the restored nation. His task was to prepare his people for the experience of the disaster of the fall of Judah and the certainty of the restoration of a disciplined people. It was the right of Isaiah (40—66) to describe the evangelistic thrust of the returned people who were challenged to become the servant of Yahweh and to suffer vicariously the persecutions of the heathen in order to win them to Yahweh and his salvation (Isa. 52:12 to 53:13).

There are some twenty-seven quotations of the Book of Jeremiah in the New Testament, not including the additional twenty-seven to be found in the Book of Revelation. The more important quotations appear to be Jeremiah 7:11; 9:22; 31:15; and, most important, 31:31-34. Indeed, the theme and development of the New Covenant of Jeremiah in the New Testament are the very essence of the Christian faith. We have the privilege of experiencing this New Covenant fulfilled in Jesus Christ.

Jeremiah's Call and Inaugural Visions
1:1-19

Superscription (1:1-3)

These introductory words are written in the third person and were added by an editor of the writings of Jeremiah. They provide the reader with information concerning Jeremiah and the period of his activity. Jeremiah was the son of Hilkiah (a name borne by nine other biblical characters and not to be confused with the contemporary high priest; compare 2 Kings 14:20; 22:3 ff.). He was of priestly lineage, undoubtedly a lineal descendent of the high priest Abiathar, who was deposed by Solomon from his office and settled in Anathoth (1 Kings 2:26). It is to be noted that Jeremiah dwelt in Benjamin rather than in Judah, although his ministry was largely centered in the capital. His early life in Anathoth is reflected in his deep affection for the north.

Jeremiah labored as a statesman and prophet from the thirteenth year of King Josiah (627 BC) until the end of the Judean state under Zedekiah in 586 BC, a ministry of some forty-one years. After this he was dragged into Egypt by Judean emigrants fleeing to escape the reprisals of Nebuchadnezzar for the murder of the newly-appointed governor Gedaliah (43:6 ff.).

His Call, Consecration, and Commission (1:4-10)

Understanding the profound significance of the call experience requires two inquiries. First we must understand the basic definition of such a call; then the other prophetic calls should be compared. The basic notion of a prophetic call can be deduced from the commissioning of the servant of Abraham to find a wife for Isaac (Gen. 24). The essential idea is that of an apostle, one sent on a mission and dispatched with a purpose, with instructions as to where and when, how and why he should proceed. The comparative examination of other prophetic calls, such as those of Moses, Isaiah, Ezekiel, and others, reveals a pattern that generally involves six parts: confrontation, salutation, commission, objection, reassurance, and pledge of support. While each call has its individuality, it has also unmistakable similarities.

The confrontation (vv. 4-5) is expressed in these words: "The word of Yahweh *was to me* saying . . ." (AT). Now there are many words in Hebrew that mean "come" or "go," but they are not used here. Rather the verb "to be" plus the preposition "to" are employed. This suggests that the word was received and perceived inwardly, distilled within the categories of his mind, expressed in his own words rather than outwardly and objectively. What may be here presented as an immediate and datable moment may actually be the telescoping of his growing awareness of God climaxing in his call.

The confrontation resulted from divine love, wisdom, and confidence: "I have chosen you." This is what Jesus said to his disciples, "You did not choose me, but I chose you and appointed you that you should go" (John 15:16). The choice is dictated by divine wisdom. God knows his servants. He trusts them and commits his tasks to them in full confidence.

In the confrontation there is the commission: it was the consecration to be a prophet to the nations. If Yahweh calls, it suggests, then no other vocation can be fulfilling. The task assigned was frightening in its scope, its implications, and its significance: a prophet to the nations!

The response (v. 6) was thoroughly expected. Jeremiah interposed his objection: he was but a youth; he had no persuasive gift of speech to effect such a program. Like Moses before him, Jeremiah was not seeking to escape responsibility but was concerned that such an important task might be miscarried by his limited abilities.

The reassurance (vv. 7-8) was immediate and unbelievable. Yahweh guaranteed him sufficiency for the divine purpose even though he was but a youth. The consecration was by rite and word: Yahweh reached out his hand and touched the lips of Jeremiah. It was the meeting of the divine and the human. Then came the sacramental word: "I have put my words in your mouth" (v. 9). The message would now be in the mind, the voice, the inner life of the prophet, not in the sense that Yahweh would use him as a ventriloquist's dummy but in the sense of the divine enlightenment passing through the human categories of the prophet. The word so conceived was then to have a universal relevance for nations and kingdoms in bad or in good; though it is a particular call it involves a universal concern and purpose. Jeremiah was to be the spokesman of that program which included positive and negative aspects (v. 10).

The Inaugural Visions (1:11-19)

The first vision was that of an almond rod (vv. 11-12). Jeremiah was privileged not only to hear the divine (audition), but to see the word (vision) in the symbol. Once again the word of Yahweh was to Jeremiah as an overarching confrontation. Jeremiah saw a vision of an almond branch, the meaning of which was clarified by a question and answer dialogue. Yahweh asked the prophet what he saw. The prophet replied that he saw a rod of almond (Hebrew: *shaqed*), to which Yahweh responded that he is watching (Hebrew: *shoqed*) over his word to perform it. It is a play on words to emphasize a point and impress the assertion forcefully that as the rod of almond watches for the return of spring when it sends forth its shoots, so Yahweh awaits the proper time and is mindful of his word to fulfill it in its proper season (compare the similar sentiment: "rising up early" used eleven times in Jeremiah). Yahweh is no absentee Lord, no deity who conceived the plan of the universe and then withdrew to let it fend for itself. He is concerned, integrated in the causes of mankind, and early rises to effect their accomplishments.

The second vision (vv. 13-19) is that of a boiling pot tilted toward the south, ominously threatening the inhabitants of the land with its fearful contents. In the question and answer dialogue the pot is interpreted to represent peoples from the north who will devastate the southern lands. In this disaster Judah and Jerusalem will be involved. The reason for the woe is that Yahweh is judging Judah for her defection and idolatry. In this judgment executed by alien nations and kings the conquest of Judah will be complete with her enemies in total domination.

Yahweh summoned his servant to courage (v. 17) and to ready himself to face the opposition of the Judean kings, its princes, its priests, and the people of the land. Jeremiah would experience their hostility as he exercised his ministry. Though they fight against him, they will not prevail, for Yahweh will be with his servant and transform his weakness into the likes of "a fortified city, an iron pillar, and bronze walls" (v. 18) against which his adversaries will be powerless.

The Early Oracles of Jeremiah
2:1 to 6:30

It is hardly possible to describe the contents of these chapters more particularly because of their diverse components. Generally they have been allocated to the reign of Josiah (640-609 BC) and represent in their language, literary forms, animation, movement, tonal quality, and beauty some of the finest poems in Jeremiah, equal to any like compositions in the Old Testament. Their setting appears to be in Jerusalem. They are autobiographically related with the speaker, the prophet himself. The subjects include a sustained indictment of Judah for her perpetual defection and her abysmal though unfounded optimism, and severe threatening of deserved judgment mingled with impassioned pleas to repent.

Israel's Perennial Faithlessness (2:1-37)

The Pristine Blissful Relationship (2:1-3)

Beginning with a nostalgic theme, both historically and religiously sensitive to his audience, the prophet referred to the Exodus experience when Israel was freed from her enslavement to be pledged tenderly to Yahweh. The mutual affection bound Yahweh and Israel together in bonds of love and fidelity as Israel followed her Master devotedly regardless of the dangers of the wilderness and the hardships of traversing a land not sown (Deut. 8:14 ff.). Israel was dedicated to Yahweh in holiness as the consecrated firstfruits (Ex. 23:19; Lev. 22:10) and brought woe upon any who defiled her. In his solicitous concern Yahweh protected his bride from harm as they moved out together into their great spiritual adventure.

The marriage relationship is often used to describe the affinity between Yahweh and Israel (Jer. 31:32; Isa. 54:5), and this use assumes a very important role in Hosea, Ezekiel, and Jeremiah. The Hebrew word for husband or master is *ba'al* and was applied to Yahweh as the husband of Israel (3:14, KJV), an idea which is utilized in the New Testament also to express the relationship between Christ and his church (2 Cor. 11:2). The symbolism of marriage between Yahweh and his people involves the additional ideas that, as marriage is an ethical commitment, so the relationship of Yahweh and Israel is essentially moral rather than ethnic. All unfaithfulness to the marriage contract is adultery, an offense whose judgment implies the possibility of divorce. The defection of Israel is, accordingly, often portrayed as an erring, adulterous wife and the divine rejection of sinful Israel as a divorce (3:8).

The Indictment of Israel (2:4-13)

This may be viewed as an idea taken from a court of law. The heavens are personified as the jury (v. 12). Israel is the defendant and Yahweh the prosecutor who is here presenting the charges: Israel had abandoned Yahweh despite his gracious care (vv. 4-8), and her behavior was irresponsible, exceptionable, and shocking (vv. 9-13). The plaintiff questions the accused for the reason for such singular defection. There is, of course, no legitimate answer to this question. The truth is that Israel forsook Yahweh, followed idolatrous vanity in both religion and life, and became utterly empty. Idolatry is often termed "vanity" or "emptiness" because it is the worship of nothing.

There was no reason for this desertion; rather, every consideration supported the contrary. Israel simply abandoned, forsook, and forgot Yahweh despite his loving care so expressively evident during the fateful years in the wilderness and in the provision of a good homeland in Palestine. But once in the land, Israel was attracted to other gods and to other religious practices. She lost that early attachment that would have made for greatness. The entire people were involved: priests, scribes, rulers, and prophets. All succumbed to the worship of Baal, the nature worship of the Canaanites, and degenerated to the sordid level of raw paganism.

The second charge laid against Israel was the utterly unthinkable rejection of Yahweh. The prophets often pointed out that while the heathen nations zealously clung to their worthless gods, Israel had paradoxically abandoned her living God, Yahweh, who was their true glory and the very fountain of living waters. How utterly inconceivable and stupid to hew out broken cisterns which cannot retain water (paganism), and that with strenuous labor in the process (its tyrannical service), when all the while there is a fountain of living waters available freely and fully (v. 13). Such irrationality and insensibility might well produce shock and utter dismay from the very heavens (v. 12)!

The Present Ruinous Course (2:14-19)

Slaves, whether foreign or domestic, can anticipate a hard lot; but Israel was not a slave, not a homeborn servant, yet the nation was experiencing the most austere servitude. Assyria, here referred to as "the lions," had wasted and depopulated the land of Judah. Egypt had likewise contributed to the national ruin. This intolerable situation was hardly becoming to the people of Yahweh. The truth of the matter is that Israel had cut Yahweh out of her life and had brought these disastrous circumstances upon itself, and the situation would not improve by the present worldly-wise foreign policies which seek now from Egypt, now from Assyria, political and military aid, only to be crushed by both (compare 2:36-37). The nation lacked a moral basis; it had no supportive courage; it had lost the will to struggle. Until the national wickedness was renounced, the national experience would continue to be both evil and bitter.

The Degenerate National Status (2:20-37)

The divine indictment.—The degenerate nation is here portrayed under various guises: an unruly farm animal (v. 20a); a nymphomaniac harlot (vv. 20b,33); a degenerate vine (v. 21; compare Isa. 5:2); a camel or wild ass in heat (vv. 23 ff.); apostates from Yahwism (vv. 6,8); polytheistic idolaters (vv. 26 ff.); slayers of the prophets (v. 30b) and the guiltless poor (v. 34); and persistently intractable (v. 30a).

The shallow and delusive optimism (2:20-35a).—Despite this overwhelming indictment Israel frivolously maintained its innocence. Punch lines from the populace are given as examples: "I am not defiled, I have not gone after the Baals" (v. 23). "I am innocent; surely his anger has turned from me. I have not sinned" (v. 35). Jeremiah often quoted such protestations of innocence and showy affirmations of devotion (compare 5:12; 6:14; 7:4,10; 8:6,8). The truth of the matter was that the nation thought that Yahwism was unpleasant and brought bad times ("a wilderness," "darkness," v. 31). The popular voice proclaimed its emancipation: "We are free; we will come no more to thee" (v. 31). To return to the old fashioned Yahwism and its straitlaced ways was unthinkable: "It is hopeless, for I have loved strangers, and after them I will go" (v. 25). "I will not serve" (v. 20). This self-deceptive attitude, mingled with defiance, created a false optimism and deluded them concerning the dread seriousness of their plight.

The divine judgment (2:35b-37).—Israel would experience the chastisement of her wickedness, and there is no substitute for the fear of Yahweh (the religion of Yahweh) but evil and bitterness (v. 19). In the day of their calamity, when all were pleading for Yahweh to save, they would discover that the no-gods whom they adored will afford no help. Judgment will come (v. 35) with its shame (v. 36) and dire sorrow (v. 37).

Apostasy and Penitence (3:1 to 4:4)

The Unacceptability of Insincere Repentance (3:1-5)

The first part of this poem begins with a question directed to the audience. The prophet, like Haggai (2:11 ff.), questioned his hearers concerning the law of divorce. "Is it possible, according to the law," he asked, "for a man who has divorced his wife and remarried again, to remarry his first wife?" (author's paraphrase). Well versed in the law (Deut. 24:1-4), the audience immediately responded with an emphatic negative reply: "Both people and land would be involved in abysmal pollution" (AT). The prophet then drew the conclusion: If the divine law prohibits such traffic in marriage and that involving only two couples, how much more is the conduct of Israel censurable when she has had a multiplicity of adulterous relationships? This refers of course to the unfaithful behavior with other gods and the gross prostitution of her relationship with Yahweh by her persistent idolatrous services.

The indictment is very severe: Israel, you are a whore. You practiced your adultery everywhere in the high places with the multiplied baalim. Like an avid Arab awaiting to attack the passerby in the wilderness, you missed no opportunity for harlotry and have polluted the land with the abominations of your lust. And now do you think that you can deceive me with your unfelt repentance? It will take more than empty words of a creed learned by rote (v. 4) and a much more serious view of the enormities you have committed before reconciliation is possible. I know your stubbornness: you have the unabashed brow of a harlot! You have not heeded the menacing lesson of judgment in the drought (v. 3a)—a view of the sympathetic interaction between nature and morality which the ancients held. You speak ever so piously, but actually you have excelled in evil (v. 5).

Faithless Israel More Faithful than Faithless Judah (3:6-18)

That this section is written in prose with the exception of verses 12-14; that it interrupts the sequence of thought in verses 1-5 and continued in verse 19; and that it deals in positive terms of a glowing future for the whole of Israel suggest that it may have been added by a later disciple of Jeremiah.

An oracular indictment (3:6-11).—This section begins with an oracle of Jeremiah uttered in the days of Josiah that expands on the defection of the Northern Kingdom in its devotion to the nature cult. Throughout its extended service to this idolatrous religion there was never a semblance of repentance, and the nation ended in 722 BC in senseless apostasy.

Judah, the Southern Kingdom, witnessed the defection, the degeneration, and the final debacle of her sister nation to the north but instead of taking heed to avoid such a disastrous course, Judah pursued the same policies with greater abandon. She witnessed that Yahweh had divorced Israel from her relationship to him (v. 8), but that tragedy did not deter Judah from her impious ways. Judah also never truly experienced a repentant attitude in all the history of her harlotries. The conclusion may be drawn: Judah did not profit from the bad example of Israel and exceeded in vileness the Northern Kingdom that met such a terrible fate; therefore, Judah is the more wicked and more severely to be judged (v. 11).

Turning then to the Northern Kingdom, the prophet called it to repentance and to the assurance of divine forgiveness because of the merciful character of Yahweh. Since all forgiveness involves contrition of heart and inward confession of wrong, the prophet urged the Northern Kingdom (now a severely reduced population under Mesopotamian domination) to acknowledge her sin and to come in truth and in faithfulness to experience the divine forgiveness (vv. 12 ff.).

The divine invitation to return (3:12-18).—A most important Hebrew term is used positively some 1,056 times in the Old Testament to mean "turn" or "return," that is, repent; or it may be used negatively to mean "turn aside," "apostatize," "become faithless." In 3:1 to 4:2, a matter of twenty-six verses, the term or a related word occurs fourteen times, creating a ringing quality in its repetition and forcefully challenging the audience: assert or desert; choose conversion or diversion.

The invitation encompasses both kingdoms: "Return, O faithless children, for I am your [husband] master [that is, I am wed to you]" (v. 14). There was a relationship so deep that not even the abundance of the national scandal could erase it, a relationship vividly portrayed in Hosea's reconciliation with his wife Gomer which as an earthly example signified the more profound relationship between Yahweh and his wayward people (compare Hos. 3:16 ff.; 11:8 ff.; 14:1 ff.).

There then follow added promises not merely of divine forgiveness but a return of the remnant now scattered far and wide to Zion (v. 14). Moreover, the forecast is promised that rulers ("shepherds") will arise to govern the restored community with enlightenment (v. 15). In that day the ark of the covenant (Ex. 25:10 ff.), the most sacred piece of furniture in the tabernacle and revered as the throne of Yahweh (compare Ps. 80:1), will lose its importance because religion will become personal and immediate, an "I-Thou" experience, not an "I-it" confrontation. The ark will be supplanted by the presence of Yahweh, a presence not merely in Israel but in the midst of the nations (v. 17). That presence will be available for all nations, who with deep ethical motivation will disown their former stubborn malpractices. At that time Israel and Judah will again be one and shall emerge from the nations to return homeward to the Land of Promise (v. 18).

This portion of Scripture (vv. 6-18) contains some cardinal doctrines of the Old Testament such as the divine purpose of Israel, the reunion of the two nations, the relative put-down of the cultic, the unity of the nations effected by the espousal of Yahwism with its ethical profile, the occupation of the Land of Promise finally realized by Israel with benign rulers to lead with understanding and knowledge. While these goals are concretely expressed, their essential meaning and fulfillment will transcend the form of expression and become the real and essential fulfillment of history (compare Heb. 11:13-16).

Penitence (3:19 to 4:4)

These verses can be broken down into three smaller units: (1) a divine monologue, 3:19-20; (2) a penitential liturgy, 3:21 to 4:2; and (3) a national exhortation, 4:3-4. In the divine monologue Yahweh muses on the tragedy of Israel and confesses the disappointment of his hopes. He wanted the nation to be his people. He wanted to favor it with a beautiful heritage for its homeland. Yahweh wanted them to experience an unswerving faithfulness, and to hear the loving invocation of his name, "My Father." All this had been dashed into pieces by Israel's unfaithfulness.

Penitential liturgies were often penned by the Israelite prophets to teach the way of repentance and to encourage its performance (compare Mic. 6:6 ff.; Hos. 14). The prophet heard the lament of his people from the "bare heights" regretting their perverted ways and shocking ingratitude with weeping and pleas (v. 21). A divine oracle beckons the penitent to return, despite unfaithfulness, and be assured of healing (v. 22*a, b*). The people now speak. The gracious invitation was accepted with the liturgical words of affirmation (v. 22*c, d*) after which followed the renunciation of paganism and the affirmation of Yahweh as the salvation of Israel (v. 23). The confession is that baalism ("the shameful thing") had ruined both heritage and people and that from the very start of the nation (v. 24 ff.). Yahweh spoke the concluding words of the liturgy by indicating that repentance involves a turning toward God and the removal of all that is offensive to that relationship. If the national life is devoted to truth, justice, and uprightness as matters of ultimate value (the oath is sworn by the highest good, compare Heb. 6:13), then the fulfillment of Israel as the messianic nation will be realized and all the nations shall bless themselves in Israel. This is the historical fulfillment of the call of Abraham (Gen. 11:3,7; 18:18; 22:18; 26:24) and the goal of biblical history.

The National Exhortation (4:3-4)—Addressed to Judah and Jerusalem, this contains three themes: an agricultural procedure (v. 3); circumcision (v. 4a); and an ominous threat (v. 4b).

The agricultural motif suggests that the national life was unfulfilled; it was not reaching its potential. Indeed, it was like a fallow field. It needed to be serviced by plowing and judicious sowing. It had potential, but this must be realized by the hard labor of farming. Then, and only then, will it reward its cultivator richly. The inference to Judah is clear.

Circumcision was a dedicatory rite that ideally indicated commitment to Yahweh. It was an outward sign of an inward reality. The prophet urged that the devotion be centered exclusively in Yahweh and that the sacrament be realized in the expression of the heart.

If the field is left untilled and if circumcision is but a bodily mutilation, then nonfulfillment and a nonfulfilling relationship with Yahweh would result and ultimately bring its judgment because of the resultant evil (v. 4).

Judgment from the North (4:5-31)

The two poems that constitute this portion of the oracle describe somewhat similarly the terrifying effect the approach of the foe from the north had made on the Southern Kingdom. Whether the Scythian, or more likely the Babylonian invasion is the subject, the alarm of the advancing enemy paralyzed all. The fear produced by the sound of the trumpet's alarm and the civil defense wardens' hastening the people to the fortified cities fairly petrified the populace (compare for similar portrayals: 47:1-3; 48:2-6; 49:23 f.). Since Jerusalem was the royal capital, affording the maximum security, the refugees were hastened there before the foe arrived (v. 6).

The poet then turned to the invader: he was like a lion with all the ferocity and strength of the king of beasts. The lion was the emblem of the Mesopotamian kings. His plundering raids resembled the ruin of the cities and the destruction of the people by the invincible armies of Babylon. The fitting response in such finality can only be to appeal to heaven, to lament and wail, to petition mercy from the

Most High despite the seemingly unending wrath.

Judah Will Fall (4:5-10)

The first poem is concluded by a prose oracle which predicts that in the day when the land is ultimately delivered into the hand of the pagans, Judah will experience a failure of nerve in king and clergy. King and prince, priest and prophet have been utterly deceived by a shallow, false optimism and have grounded their policies accordingly. The threatened invasion demanded a complete reversal of all they had thought and purposed. The Judean leaders had committed themselves to the wrong cause and had played into the hands of their unmerciful enemy from the north. Verse 10 should read not "Then I said . . .," but rather "And they shall say . . .," that is, the optimistic and misguided priests and prophets.

A Devastating Invasion (4:11-18)

The second poem (vv. 11-18) begins in prose (vv. 11-12) and then switches into poetry. In the opening clause an identity with the same setting as the preceding oracle of woe may be fairly deduced. The actual composition begins with the words: "A hot wind . . . " and proceeds to describe the devastation of the invasion under the figure of a burning desert wind (the sirocco) which sears the land with its heat. Yahweh is the narrator of the ravages of the hostile foe as he strode uncontested through the land.

More particularly, the enemy pursued his thrust with the speed of the clouds; his chariots were like the whirlwind, his horses swifter than eagles (v. 13). The imminent danger elicited from Yahweh an injunction to Jerusalem to wash her heart from wickedness, a last call in the desperate time, suggesting an untimely late rescue. But this aside, verse 14 slows only momentarily the woeful distress of the invasion. From Dan in the north to Mount Ephraim there is nothing but ominous news (v. 15). The urgency of the moment is to warn the nations (more particularly, Jerusalem), to be prepared to meet the foreign besiegers who encircle their quarries with battle shouts. This poem concludes mournfully that the evil ways of the nation have generated this bitter woe, a woe that reaches the very heart.

The Alarm of War (4:19-22)

The third poem appears as a dialogue between Jeremiah (vv. 19-21) and Yahweh (v. 22). It is not unusual for a prophet to identify himself with the woes of his people (compare 8:21; Mic. 1:8 f.), but none empathize so pathetically as Jeremiah. First, he gave free vent to his pent-up grief at the devastating alarm of the foe's approach toward Judah (v. 19). The intensity of his anguish was marked by nominal repetition expressed without predicate: "My anguish, my anguish!" This is then analyzed in the words: "I writhe in pain!"

Again, the subject was blurted out, "Oh, the walls of my heart!" followed by the agitated words: "My heart is beating wildly." Under such nervous duress he could not be silent as again and again the sound of the trumpet, the alarm of war was heard (vv. 19,21). Disaster followed disaster upon the devastated land. His personal fortunes (pictured in the symbols of his tent) were fragmented overnight. The lament ends with a formula so expressive, so often found in the psalms of lament. It is the unanswerable question: How long? How long must the standard be seen? How long must the trumpet sound? Some ancient Sumerian laments repeat this question "How long . . .?" a dozen or more times; it finds expression in the Akkadian laments and in the biblical psalms (Pss. 4:3; 35:17; 74:10).

The response of Yahweh to this passionate outcry of Jeremiah laid bare the good reason for the disastrous days: "My people are foolish, without knowledge; stupid without understanding. Skilled, indeed, in doing evil, but ignorant how to do good" (v. 22, AT; compare Isa. 1:16 ff.).

The Chaotic Situation (4:23-28)

This unbearably tragic hour was for Jeremiah reminiscent of the turbulence before the creation (Gen. 1:2). There was naught in the present state of affairs but waste and void. No light was seen in the quivering mountains, no man, no bird, nothing but endless desert. So the ruined country with its cities in shambles, forsaken of man and beast, reminded Jeremiah of the chaos in the beginning. The oracle ends with a tiny word of hope, that despite the seeming unrelieved tragedy there will not be a full end, a total destruction (v. 27). However, God will not turn back from his punishment (v. 28).

Invasion, Censure, and Demise (4:29-31)

The final oracle pictures the invading cavalry and archers before whom the cities fly to the thicket and caverns to find safety (v. 29). Yet amid the gravity of the situation Judah continued her harlotry with cosmetic blandishments and fetching clothing in the hope of finding security from her lovers. All was done in vain (v. 30). Her lovers (foreign allies) despised her and sought her life, so that Zion was like a pregnant woman in birth pangs, little realizing that death was near at the hands of her former lovers now turned enemies. The imagery is allegorical. It portrays the vain attempt of Judah to improve her political profile so that the nation may gain military support from her neighbors. But they would not accept the overtures. They used her when it served their purpose and murdered her when it proved expedient (compare Lam. 1:7 ff.; 2:16). Seeking political favors involved the prostitution of the nation's religious code and proved rewardless.

Judah's Guilty Iniquity (5:1 to 6:30)

An Unavailing Inquiry (5:1-5)

The prophet was commanded to search diligently throughout Jerusalem to see if there was a righteous man, for if found, Yahweh would free the city of blame (v. 1). Knowing the evil leanings of his people so well, Jeremiah suggested indirectly that the search would prove useless; they were perjurers, insensible, unchanging, adamant, and impenitent (vv. 2 ff.). His first mission to seek a righteous man among the poor was a complete failure; one and all were ignorant both of religion and ethics (v. 4). Turning then to the upper level of society where it might be anticipated that a righteous man might be located, Jeremiah discovered that they, too, were no improvement over the poor. All were like an unruly farm animal kicking over the traces (v. 5).

The Inevitable Judgment (5:6-9)

The rigorous punishment will now accord with the transgressions. It will exact its fearful toll and will meet the people as the three named beasts ferociously encounter their quarry (v. 6). Pardon is unthinkable. Apostasy, idolatry, and adultery spell nothing but national judgment (vv. 7-9).

Matters That Have Invited Disaster (5:10-17)

Yahweh issued an order to destroy the false branches from his "vine-rows" (v. 10; compare 2:21; Isa. 5:2,4). The reason is then added: the alien branches represent unfaithfulness, humanistic optimism falsely begotten, and the rejection of the prophetic word, all of which must be rejected (vv. 11-13). However, the words of the prophets are not optional. In Jeremiah's mouth the words are a fire, and the people will be the wood—and the conflagration the judgment (v. 14). The devouring holocaust will be the invaders of the land who are from an enduring and ancient nation. They speak a foreign tongue, but their warfare is lethal, their economic reprisals devastating, and their destruction of military strongholds complete (vv. 15-17; compare Deut. 28:49).

A Commentary on the Times (5:18-19)

The assertion of Jeremiah was to the effect that though the judgment be ever so severe, it would not be the total end of the people (v. 18). This thesis is repeated (4:27; 5:10,18) and softens the sterner judgmental utterances (13:13 ff.). The question-answer that follows is the justification for the Exile; it is because of the defection of Israel (v. 19; 9:12-14; 16:10,13; 22:8 ff.). The same thought is elsewhere to be found in the Old Testament (Deut. 29:24 ff.; 1 Kings 9:8 ff.).

Judah's Boundless Transgression (5:20-31)

Very solemnly the prophet was to charge the nation with its crimes (vv. 20-25). The audience was addressed in disgraceful epithets: fools and brainless, possessed (spiritually) of blind eyes and deaf ears (compare Isa. 6:9). Then follow two questions, one interrogation: Do you have no religion at all? The restless sea has its bounds, but this people observed no limits; theirs was nothing but a stubborn and rebellious heart. They were never moved with gratitude to the Most High; and such thanklessness destroyed the possibility of all human fulfillment (vv. 20-25).

Moreover, the people were captured like birds by the enterprising wicked who prospered in their boundless iniquity. The wicked had no sense of justice or righteousness. Pity was foreign to their thinking. Shall not such abnormal behavior be dealt with in Yahweh's earth (v. 29)? And yet, despite all this total disharmony, a more appalling and horrible situation arose: the prophets prophesied falsely, the priests obtained power at their hands, and Yahweh's people loved to have it so (vv. 30-31). But then comes the fearful conclusion: What will you do when the end comes (compare

9:9)? The connivance of the priest and the prophet was notorious in
Israel (v. 31; 6:13 ff.; 23:9-22; Mic. 3:5-8).

The Invasion Alarm Sounded in Judah (6:1-8)

The prophet warned the Benjaminites who had taken refuge in
Jerusalem to abandon that stronghold for some other more secure
refuge. He summoned the city of Tekoa and the neighboring town of
Beth-haccherem to raise the alarm because of the evil that was
imminent from the north (v. 1). Words spoken either by Yahweh or
the northern commanders indicated the unopposable destruction
that would be wreaked upon Zion (v. 2). Around the city would be
the military encampments of the enemy (v. 3), stationed there to
formulate by day or by night the most strategic plan of attack
(vv. 4-5).

An oracle of Yahweh now begins: it was the divine word of
judgment to the invaders to build siege mounds against Jerusalem
in order to punish the city for her continuing wickedness and her
sickness unto death (v. 6 ff.). It concludes with an admonition, so it
would seem, to Jerusalem to be warned of the dire situation and
suggests a repentant mood (v. 8).

Justification for the Invasion (6:9-15)

This second portion of the chapter begins with the order of
Yahweh to the invaders to glean the remnant of Israel (v. 9; compare
5:10). The prophet continued the oracle by indicating its justification: the people refused to listen to the divine word which had
become an object of scorn in their eyes, and they wholly displeased
Yahweh (v. 10). Whether it be Yahweh or the prophet himself, more
likely the latter, he was filled with indignation with his people and
weary of suppressing his exasperation (v. 11). He unfolded what the
wrath of Yahweh would be to the sinful people: it included all ages
and all possessions in its fearful sweep (v. 12). Coveteousness for
unjust gain infected the entire population, particularly those expected to be above it—the prophet and the priest—who with their
false prescriptions and shallow optimism proclaimed "Peace,
peace," when there was no peace! They were callously unashamed
of their abomination; consequently, their doom was deserved and
certain (vv. 13-15). This benediction of the clergy (v. 14b) so
hypocritically given to the people appears by its repetition in 8:11-12

to have been a significant part of the cultic worship and was indicative of the baseless optimism of their priestly power much as the meaningless cry, "The temple of the Lord, the temple of the Lord" (7:4).

The Will of the Lord (6:16-21)

The oracle summoned the people to the good old ways wherein was rest for the soul (v. 16); but the invitation was rejected. Again the divine warnings sounded the coming dangers, but these too were summarily discounted. It follows then that, if the people did not wish the good, all that was left was evil and the fruits of their disobedience (v. 20). The sacrificial cult with its incense and offerings afforded no substitute for obedience. It may pacify the deluded conscience for the moment but will not prevent the divine judgment (v. 21; compare 7:21-23). Yahweh would lay stumbling blocks before the disobedient which would occasion their fall. The stumbling blocks were those matters that delight God, that is, the ethical code such as the Ten Commandments. But the people were repelled by these; they wanted to do their own thing, in their own way, and took offense at the divine desires. Strange that that which God meant for mankind's good should become objectionable and a stumbling block (v. 21; compare Isa. 8:14 ff.; Matt. 16:23; 1 Cor. 1:23).

The Foe from the North Again (6:22-26)

In this frightful oracle the foe from the north was described in his advance toward the land of Judah with his superb weaponry and cavalry (vv. 22-23). The scene then rapidly changed to those who heard the woeful news of the invasions: they were paralyzed with fear, their mobility was restricted by enemy infiltration, and bitter lamentation was the only recourse of the bewildered as they faced the sudden attack of the destroyer (v. 26).

The Prophet, the Tester of the People (6:27-30)

Jeremiah was to determine the true value of his people and their ways. The test showed that they were uniformly rebellious, slanderers, brazen, and corrupt. However long the refining, however much lead was added to separate the precious from the base, the result was the same. The impurities were not removed; nothing but refuse silver remained, and that was valueless scrap (v. 30; compare

Isa. 1:22*a*; Ezek. 22:17). "Refuse silver" is what they would be called; what else could Yahweh do but refuse them?

Prophecies Largely from the Time of Jehoiakim
7:1 to 20:18

The Sermon on the Temple (7:1-15)

After a divine injunction to deliver the oracle to the Judeans as they entered the gates of the Temple, the prophet enjoined the people to change their ways and abandon the hope falsely coined by the priests that the Temple would ensure the safety of the country (vv. 1-4). The words of Jeremiah 26:4-6 are closely parallel, which by superscription are dated in the reign of Jehoiakim. One can feel the fanatical confidence of the Judeans in the false assurance of Judah's invincibility by virtue of the presence of Yahweh in the Temple. It would be unthinkable for him to be overcome by the heathen enemy; accordingly, the people and the land were safe and secure.

The prophet conceded that if there was a radical correction of their ways with justice prevailing, with concern for the bereft, with murder ceasing, and with idolatry removed, then the Judeans might confidently hope to abide in the land (vv. 5-7). But, continued Jeremiah, everything tended to point in the other direction. A false confidence in what Yahweh would do and would not do had fooled the people to such an extent that after having committed theft, adultery, perjury, and idolatrous service, they had the nerve to address Yahweh with the profession, "We are delivered"—only to contradict their words by renewed abominable practices (vv. 8-11). What kind of a house do you imagine the Temple to be? Is my house a harbor for thieves (compare Ps. 50:16-18)? I know full well what is going on. Your impious confidence will prove your undoing, as devastating a disappointment as your ancestors, who similarly trusted in the tabernacle at Shiloh (1 Sam. 4—6; Ps. 78:56-72), felt when Yahweh abandoned his dwelling to the ravages of the enemy.

Jesus uttered similar solemn words: "Behold, your house is forsaken and desolate" (Matt. 23:38; compare Jer. 12:7; 22:5). The constant refusal to hearken to Yahweh will occasion not merely the destruction of the beloved Temple but an exile like that of their kinsmen Israel (v. 15).

Perversions in Worship and Divine Judgment (7:16 to 10:25)

The Idolatrous Astral Worship (7:16-20)

Jeremiah was admonished not to intercede for the people who were occupied with the service of Astarte (Ishtar), the queen of heaven. The entire family—father, mother, and children—devoted their efforts to the liturgy of this well-known goddess and other foreign gods (compare 44:15-28). Here, asserted Jeremiah, was confusion compounded. The people did not make Yahweh mad; they were mad themselves, and the end was destruction (v. 20).

Obedience More than Sacrifice (7:21-28)

The sacrificial cult was often regarded as an end in itself: merely perform the act, speak the correct word, and automatically the sought blessing was won. Such religious practice was divorced from ethical considerations and thus from God himself. The officiating priest, the offerer, and the central meaning of the rite, according to this view, had nothing to do with the power of the sacrifice to work. Only the doing of the rite mattered, without regard to its ethical character. Such was the practiced reasoning among the people in the time of Jeremiah.

But there were other considerations that militated against such empty ritualism. Jeremiah suggested ironically that the people continue to do their practices: to add burnt offerings to sacrifices, then eat the sacrificial meat. This was as firmly entrenched in their religious observances as was their custom to repeat ad nauseam: "The temple of the Lord." The fact of the matter was that when Yahweh brought Israel out of Egypt, he said nothing about sacrifices. What he did speak about was primary and essential: Israel was to obey his voice and thereby establish fellowship between themselves and their God. The word was solely about obedience. That indispensable obedience had fallen into disuse, and that which was foreign to the intent of the divine confrontation with Israel, namely, ritualism, had assumed the illegitimate primacy. With all their sacrifices Israel was an ethical failure. The nation had missed the entire point of religion. They had walked in the waywardness of their own idolatrous heart, far removed from Yahweh. From the very day of the Exodus till now Yahweh had solicited the obedience of his people, but the nation had persistently refused to obey and consistently degenerated for the worse (vv. 21-26). It was not sacrifice, not ritual; it was obedience and fellowship Yahweh sought—something that Israel never quite understood. That this concept of ethical religion gripped the heart of Jeremiah and constituted a foundational belief in his thought may be gathered from the fact that its expression in 7:23-28 is repeated in 11:1-7.

Enormities in the Valley of Hinnom (7:29-34)

The prophet called the nation to raise a lamentation with its accompanying customs because Yahweh had rejected his people (v. 29; compare Mic. 1:8; Joel 1:13 ff.; 2:15-17). There follows the grave indictment of child sacrifice in the valley of the son of Hinnom, close to the walls of Jerusalem, a practice that was utterly foreign and revolting to Yahweh (v. 31). The oracle concludes with the solemn prediction that the valley will one day be filled with corpses so as to merit a new name, that of the valley of Slaughter, because of the abominable practice perpetrated upon the helpless children. No more shall the normal joy and gladness of the people flourish here; the land will become a waste (v. 34).

Sacrilege and Doom (8:1-3)

The previous oracle had condemned the evil rite of child sacrifice (7:31). An addition to that word of judgment here predicted that a kindred fate would befall the kings, princes, priests, prophets, and people of Judah when their tombs would be rifled and their bones profanely strewn everywhere. It would be a suitable fate, fitting for those who offered their children to the astral deities, to be immediately exposed to the sun, moon, and heavenly bodies as refuse, an appropriate and contemptuous emblem both of their worship and their moral worth (8:1-2). In that day death would be preferred to life wherever the remnant of the Judeans flees (v. 3).

It must be borne in mind that burial was sacred and that those that pillaged a tomb were guilty of a crime of immense magnitude

(Amos 2:1-3). Tombs were erected to protect and preserve the remains of the deceased. To have one's tomb desecrated was unthinkable. Yet the astral devotees who sacrificed their children, either for oracular purpose or for a greater chance for the gods to act, would be unprotected by the heavenly host from such sacrilege, despite their unbounding religious fanaticism.

Judah's Inconsequential Behavior (8:4-7)

Two situations are presented here, involving appropriate action in each case. If one falls, does one not rise? If one turns away, say, on a journey, does one not return? In both instances the individual responds intelligently. Why, then, asked Yahweh, do this people, having turned away, not return to me (compare 3:7)? Paradoxically, they keep on going in perpetual apostasy and evil. Though warned, none return; none repents of his evil ways. Like a horse plunging headlong into battle, the Judeans recklessly, impetuously pursue their evil course. Even the stork knows the time of her nesting, the turtledove, swallow, and crane the time of their migration. But my people, lamented Yahweh, do not know the divine ordinances. They appear inadequate to make the right response.

Perversion of Yahweh's Law (8:8-12)

This section (vv. 8-9) is followed by a censure of the prophets and priests for their false optimism and shallow view of morality, with an appropriate fate forecast for them (vv. 10-12). These three verses are duplicated in 6:12-15, and the commentary is given there. It may have been that these verses were inserted here to bring together the three religious groups responsible for much of the evil of the times.

Scribalism and the perversion of the law compose the subject of verses 8-9. The introductory sentence is a punch line among the scribes. It affirms two matters: first, the rather arrogant self-opinion of this professional group; and second, the allegation of their authority stemming from their vocation. This vaunted assertion is questioned: How can you say this, "We are wise, and the law of the Lord is with us?" (v. 8). The fact of the matter is quite otherwise: you scribes are unwise; and the law of Yahweh is not with you. The second part of verse 8 substantiates this allegation. The scribes were the ancient lawyers and, as such, were interpreters of the law whether religious, civil, or criminal. Law is one thing; interpretation is quite another. Throughout recorded history the law courts have been tainted with perennial guilt. By an addition here and a deletion there, by an emphasis here and a slight there, they have perverted the law (religion/tradition) into a lie (compare a similar charge in Matt. 15:3 ff.; Mark 7:8-13). As Paul phrased it, "Professing themselves to be wise, they became fools, And changed . . . " (Rom. 1:22, KJV). Here the scribes rejected the law of Yahweh, which was ultimate wisdom, and made up their own law from their foolishness. Nothing could be expected but disaster, and that was predicted to arrive.

The Barren Fruitage (8:13)

This verse illustrates the fragmentary nature of the writings of Jeremiah. It hardly agrees in subject with that which precedes or follows. It is an expression of the pathetic disappointment of Yahweh to have found no fruitage in his vineyard (compare Isa. 5:2,4; Mark 11:12 ff.; Luke 13:6 ff.) or his fig tree; even worse, the leaves were withered and the investment diminished. Naturally it has reference to Yahweh's disappointment with the behavior of the Judeans.

The Judean Frustration (8:14-15)

In this monologue the people of Judah gave vent to their sorry plight. There was an undercurrent of resentment against the harsh fate decreed by Yahweh. The moment demanded immediate action. They planned to assemble and seek security within the fortified cities, but the feeling everywhere was that this was futile. To perish in the fortresses appeared to be Yahweh's judgment. The Judeans admitted that they had sinned against Yahweh. Nevertheless, they looked for peace and national well-being. Alas, nothing good happened, nothing but terror.

At times Jeremiah protested the Judeans' immorality, a judgment that applied to all the people. Here is an instance in which there was a pathetic empathy in Jeremiah's words at the sorrowful impasse of his people. The people had no hope at all. To take refuge in the fortified cities was to perish, if not by the foe then some other way equally abhorrent. That seemed to be the inflexible command of heaven. But if the people had sinned, was there no eternal mercy, no measure of peace, however small, no healing? The sympathies of Jeremiah seem here to be identified with his people's oppressive and inescapable lot.

The Invaders from the North (8:16-17)

Yahweh disclosed the judgment upon the Judeans: it would come from the foe from the north, which with excited horses was speedily invading the land from Dan, the northern border of ancient Israel. Beneath the ferocious hordes the whole land fairly quaked, and for good reason: the foe could not be stopped. It resembled snakes which could not be wooed ("charmed") from their deadly mission.

A Trio of Despair (8:18-22)

Three participate in this fragmentary composition: Jeremiah (vv. 18-19,21), Yahweh (v. 19*e,f*), and the people (vv. 19*c,d*,20-21). A pathetic outcry of Jeremiah indicated the measure of his inward grief (v. 18). His identity with his suffering people sensitized his feelings for their plight and for their misunderstanding of the grave situation (v. 19*c,d*). Yahweh responded to the rhetorical questions of the frustrated people with two questions of his own. These questions clearly demonstrate that Yahweh and the nation are on two different wave lengths. Of what benefit is the union of the divine and evil? What can result from Yahweh being in Zion and the nation living in sin? Jeremiah then recorded the pessimistic saying, no doubt current at the time, that "The harvest is past, the summer is ended, and we are not saved" (v. 20). This saying is logically divided: the first two lines are prefatory; the last line, the punch line, startled the hearer. It was the unexpected outcome of the premises; it was not the way things should be. Here is used the literary figure where one anticipated one conclusion and was rudely shocked by another. The expressive proverb may be translated as "missing the boat." Jeremiah added his sad unity with his people's situation: they are a sick people; he cannot abandon them; their problem is his problem.

Jeremiah often used medical terms to express religious ideas (15:18; 30:15), a deep insight into the psychosomatic nature of mankind. The positive side of medicine is employed in the concluding words of this section, in which three questions are urged. The rhetorical question is often an emphatic declarative, as it is here. The affirmations are these: there is balm in Gilead; there is a physician available; the health (literally, proud flesh) of my daughter could have, should have been restored (literally, gone up, the healthy state of skin that has formed a scar). Yahweh's people had a serious wound. The medical facilities and personnel were there. Why, then, is she not healed?

A Pathetic Lament for Judah (9:1-3)

In 8:21 and following, Jeremiah empathized with his desperately ill people. Now he gave free expression to his emotion and, as he viewed their coming catastrophe, wished for sufficient tears to lament befittingly (v. 1). With the sorrow oppressing beyond endurance he longed to escape far from the tragic scene—to the desert, to a wayfarers' lodge. Such escape fantasy was induced by the enormity of the sin of his people: adultery, treachery, falsehood, to name a few, worsening and progressive, without the faintest knowledge of Yahweh (v. 3). The knowledge of Yahweh is not primarily intellectual; it is moral and contrasted here with the vices mentioned.

A Warning Against the Faithless Judeans (9:4-6)

Turning from his own disappointment and sorrow, he urged his fellow Judeans to beware of each other as bad risks. So treacherous are they that even in a neighbor, nay, in a brother, one should put no trust. They were deceivers and liars, multiplying oppression and deceit and refusing to know Yahweh.

An Oracle to Justify the Judgment (9:7-9)

The order of thought has led from indictment to judgment. Because the Judeans were utterly treacherous even to their neighbors and their words nothing but deceit, Yahweh would place them in the crucible, to refine and test his people—a hard prospect but the only alternative to the present situation. And it was forecast that on such a nation as had been described, this punishment would result.

The Lamentation over Judah (9:10-11)

In this oracle Yahweh called for a proper lament to be taken up over the desolated and ruined land and forecasted the destruction of Jerusalem and Judah.

Justification of Judah's Demise (9:12-16)

This section is a takeoff on the question-answer instructional pattern used by the scribes or wise men. Two questions initiate the dialogue; both are concerned with the correct answer as to why the land is ruined and depopulated (v. 12). The reason is then provided by Yahweh: the inhabitants had forsaken Yahweh and walked in the conceits of their own hearts; they had practiced idolatry like their wayward forebears and had brought upon themselves this judgment of Yahweh. This judgment is graphically described as a bitter pill to swallow as well as involving a scattering of Judah among the nations, relentlessly pursued by the sword of justice (vv. 15 ff.)

A Communal Lament for Judah (9:17-22)

Yahweh summoned skillful people to conduct an appropriate lament with wailing and tears, with a poignant text over the ruin of Zion and the deportation of the people. The future reality of these disasters is presented as having already occurred (vv. 17-19). The second part of the oracle is a dirge, a funereal lament for the slain of the populace with death everywhere, indiscriminate in its selection and multiplied like sheaves after a reaper or resembling dung upon the open field (vv. 20-22).

The True Wisdom of the Wise Man (9:23-24)

In prose and expressed in a different mood, Yahweh urged the wise man not to glory in his wisdom, the mighty man not to glory in his might, and the rich man not to glory in his wealth. Instead he should glory that he knew Yahweh, a God who practiced and delighted in kindness, justice, and righteousness in the earth. Once again the knowledge of Yahweh is defined and is extolled as man's ultimate achievement. Men prize most highly the possession of riches, wisdom, and power. Nevertheless these pale in insignificance when compared with the knowledge of Yahweh, a much more rewarding acquisition for one's ultimate goal in life. Paul used the thought and a portion of this significant selection in his Corinthian letters (1 Cor. 1:20-31; 2 Cor. 10:17).

True Circumcision (9:25-26)

Unfortunately, the translations of the King James Version and Revised Standard Version seem meaningless; accordingly, another version will be presented, and the reader will be able to grasp the point of this extremely important affirmation on a sensitive subject.

Lo, days are coming—declares the Lord—when I will take note of everyone circumcised in the foreskin: of Egypt, Judah, Edom, the Ammonites, Moab, and all the desert dwellers who have the hair of

their temples clipped. All these nations are uncircumcised [just as] all
the House of Israel are uncircumcised of heart. (AT)

Once again Jeremiah repudiated the external: biology, ethnology,
nationalism are accidents; the Temple, its sacrifices, and Zion were
external to the essential meaning of religion. As Paul maintained,
circumcision is but mutilation if the inner reality is lacking.
Circumcision of the heart, that is, the embodiment of the ethical
within the inner life, is what was lacking in the house of Israel; the
bodily rite is otherwise meaningless (compare 4:4; Gal. 5:6). Israel
differed in no way from the heathen!

The Impotence of Heathenism (10:1-5)

The oracle of Yahweh enjoined Israel to studiously avoid the way
of the nations and singles out two practices, astrology (v. 2) and
idolatry (vv. 3-5), for ridicule. Astral phenomena such as an eclipse,
meteors, and the position of the planets were viewed with great
foreboding by the ancients. An involved astrology was devised to
cope with the omens divined by the astrologers. Incantations were
formulated to ward off the evils of an eclipse and were extensively
employed in Near Eastern religious practices. The other injunction
is against idolatry. This is more complicated than it seems at first
glance. Man has an urgent desire to concretize the invisible. The
pagans called the Jews atheists because they had no image of their
God (compare the Second Commandment, Ex. 20:4-6). Moreover,
the abstract does not readily lend itself to ritualism, another
fascination of mankind. People would rather see and feel than to
think and project in metaphysical symbols. Idolatry lends itself to
the sensuous, the aesthetic, the artistic. The great temptation has
always been for man to make his gods in his own image or to
represent the properties of his god in some physical representation.
Idolatry was Israel's besetting sin for centuries until the Babylonian
captivity took away their desire for idols.

The fabrication of an idol is pictured in verses 3-5. Its stock was a
tree which was carved into the supposed form of the god. It was
overlaid with silver and gold and secured from falling by suitable
fastenings. Yahweh, having described the construction of an idol,
now ironically pointed out its impotence: immobility, inability to
speak, and a laughingstock. Since idols are powerless to do anything, Yahweh exhorted, his people are not to serve idols.

A Hymn to the Incomparable God (10:6-16)

In hymnic style the psalm begins by extolling Yahweh for his incomparableness and greatness (compare Ex. 9:14; 15:11; Ps. 40:18,26 ff.), worthy of reverence as king of the nations. Compared with Yahweh and his wisdom, the wise of the nations were naive and foolish as they conjured up advice from idols. Despite the care lavished on their idols with Tarshishan silver and Uphazian gold, skillfully carved and clothed in violet and purple, they were nothing but nonentities and misrepresentations of the Divine Being. On the contrary, Yahweh is the true, the living, and the everlasting God and King, at whose indignation the earth is unequal.

The hymn is interrupted by verse 11, which strangely enough is written in Aramaic, not Hebrew, and which certainly must be regarded as an explanation originally written in the margin which later became part of the text. The affirmation appears to have been used by the Jews in captivity where Babylonian idolatry was rampant and where Aramaic was the common language.

The hymn now continues the eulogy of Yahweh by singling out his power and his wisdom in the creation and the governance of the world (v. 15). All the atmospheric phenomena are under his control: thunder, lightning, rain, mist, and wind alike (v. 13). Compared with Yahweh, man is incredibly ignorant in seeking help from his false and fabricated idols. In the divine confrontation of history they will be shown to be worthless, delusive, and disappointing. The portion of Jacob (Yahweh) is quite different: his God is the Creator, the Lord of hosts; and Israel is the tribe of his inheritance (v. 16). This hymn is repeated in 51:15-19.

A Threat of Doom (10:17-18)

The injunction is in the form of a divine oracle enjoining those under the siege to gather their belongings and join the inhabitants of the land who are being slung out into the Exile. It is a very short poem and fits in well with the prophet's lament that follows and verse 22 in which the invaders from the north spell disaster.

Reaction, Lament, and Indictment (10:19-21)

The previous verses portray a poignant scene. How could the prophet not be affected by it? In a word akin to *curse* he described his calamity, then changed the idiom to that of a grievous wound. But self-pity would not avail; Jeremiah called the pathos its right name and courageously shouldered his cross (v. 19). But one is only human, and each has one's personal set of unforgettable attachments. Life is like a tent with its bracing cords destroyed, and there is none to rebuild the structure. So pondered Jeremiah, as his mind then turned to those responsible for his personal calamity. He reprimanded the rulers ("shepherds") for their crass stupidity, their stubbornness in refusing to inquire of Yahweh. Therefore, their land is impoverished, and the ending is sure to be an exile of the population.

Three Miscellanea (10:22-25)

The first is the recurrent threat of the northern invader coming to reduce Judah to ruins (v. 22). The second fragment is a confessional prayer of profound insight, one of the masterpieces of wisdom and the profoundest of its type in Jeremiah (vv. 23-24). In a frank acknowledgment the prophet confessed that man—and he was very conscious at this point of his own manhood—is not the master of his ways, that he cannot control his behavior. One might inject the question whether Jeremiah had in mind the intrusion of the external world into the realm of the ego or self. Was it his genes, his place of origin, his cultural environment, his peer groups, his contemporary mores, his delusive and alluring opportunities laced with evil, his personal idolatries, bombarding him relentlessly, that controlled man? There are magnetisms of which he is unaware. He flies through a magnetic field with a faulty compass. Accordingly, the prophet petitioned Yahweh for the necessary correction man needs, pointing out that such correction must be done in mercy, for if done in wrath it would destroy him. It is a magnificent prayer with profound insight into the ways of man and of God, an admission of inadequacy with a prayer for sufficiency.

The last fragment is a prayer calling for a curse upon the nations who do not know Yahweh, upon the people that do not worship him (v. 25). The motivation of this petition is the deep resentment felt when these nations had devoured Jacob and laid waste his home (v. 25). The same prayer is contained in Psalm 79:6-7 and is an index of the righteous indignation in the Judean hearts against their despoilers.

The question arises in regard to the propriety of such a prayer asking for a curse. Certainly, it is a very human reaction against the outrages of having their belongings taken, a desperate cry against the inhumanity of aggression, of power against weakness, of right against wrong. All this accords with eye for eye morality (Matt. 5:43) but falls short of the teaching of the New Testament of praying for one's enemies and blessing them that despitefully use one. This ethic was quite unheard of before Christ's advent and, unfortunately, is too seldom witnessed among his followers.

The Broken Covenant (11:1-17)

This section may be divided into three parts: verses 1-5, verses 6-8, and verses 9-17. Each is introduced with an oracular notice, "[Yahweh] said to me" or the like, and each is in prose.

Exhortation to Obey the Covenant (11:1-5)

Jeremiah was told to reason with the Judeans concerning Yahweh's covenant with them. He stressed the serious business of fulfilling the demands of that covenant; for, should the nation fail, the ominous curses will follow. And contrariwise, if the covenant was maintained, the blessings would be theirs. The covenant in question is, of course, the Sinaitic covenant, and details of that event are here generally specified: the parties were Yahweh and "your fathers"; the time was when Yahweh brought them out of the land of Egypt, from a situation as intolerable as an iron furnace. The terms of the covenant are alluded to: "You shall be my people, and I will be your God" (compare Ex. 19:5; 6:7; Jer. 7:23). The curse for noncompliance may be suggested by the curses inherent in the covenant stipulations (compare Deut. 27:15 ff.; 28:15 ff.). On the other hand, a performance of the obligations of the covenant would ensure the continuity of that patriarchal promise, which would grant the Promised Land even to the harrassed Judeans in the time of Jeremiah. To the divine oracle the prophet solemnly agreed (v. 5).

A Second Call to Covenantal Loyalty (11:6-8)

From verse 6 one can guess that Jeremiah must have made an itinerant mission to the cities of Judah, as well as to the capital, urging the Judeans to renew their loyalty to the ancient covenant. The notion that Jeremiah undertook this mission as a result of the law book which was discovered in the Temple in order to urge conformity to that newly-found book seems inadequate. More likely,

Jeremiah had in mind the total covenant arrangements between Yahweh and Israel. Yet the mention of the curse in verse 3 and the menacing tone of this present passage are not dissimilar to the threatening words of the prophetess Huldah after she had read the newly-discovered book of the law in 621 BC. Yahweh reminded his straying people that from time immemorial even to the present he had urged obedience but, alas, all without result. In the stubbornness of their evil hearts Israel refused to obey and was due all the penalties involved in the broken covenant (compare 7:13,25; 25:3b; 26:5; 29:19; 35:14 ff.; 44:4). The latter part of verse 8 might better be rendered, "Therefore I am about to bring upon them," for the nation was still encouraged to change its ways and the Exile was yet to take place. The two oracles (11:1-8) are in substance akin to 7:21-26; even the same words are used in a number of instances. The subject under review was of extreme importance to the prophet and forms an essential part of his proclamation.

The Third Oracle (11:9-17)

The oracle begins with an indictment of Judah: they had copied the sins of their forebears, served other gods, and broken the covenant (vv. 9 ff.). Consequently, an inescapable judgment awaited them in which heaven would be silent to their appeals. Vainly would they petition their impotent gods, despite their multiplicity of altars. It must have been an unbearable cross for Jeremiah to witness the numerous idols Judah had incorporated in her worship. Particularly notable is the mention of Baal with its attendant nature cult.

The unyielding determination of Yahweh to punish the defection of his people necessarily involved his apostle Jeremiah. Yahweh told him not to intercede for the unrepentant people, for their prayers would be unavailing. Then amid flashbacks to happier days Yahweh takes away the Judeans' hopeful expectancy because of Judah's vile behavior. The happier flashbacks include the endearing epithet "my beloved" and the planting of the nation (v. 17) as "a green olive tree, fair with goodly fruit" (v. 16). But Judah's vileness has rightly denied her access to Yahweh's house, nor can the offered vows and sacrifices ward off her doom. Judah had nothing to plead but apostasy, vile deeds, and limitless evil. Yahweh's judgment would come as a fire fanned by a great tempest and consume the branches of the once fair olive tree. The restraint placed upon the prophet from interceding for his people must have been an added burden to the prophet.

The Plot Against Jeremiah and the First Confession
(11:18 to 12:6)

The Plot Against Jeremiah (11:18-23)

This section is part of the so-called "Confessions of Jeremiah," more particularly, part of the first Confession. These six profoundly moving and pathetic personal prayers depict the agony of the prophet as he wrestled against the oppressing problems that tormented him. The Confessions are generally identified as: (1) 11:18 to 12:6; (2) 15:10-21; (3) 17:14-18; (4) 18:18-23; (5) 20:7-13; and (6) 20:14-18. While their range is variously described by individual scholars, there is no doubt that they constitute a series of prayers unequaled in their intensity, urgency, honesty, and pathos in the Old Testament, with the possible exception of those in Job.

Written initially in poetry (vv. 18-20), then in prose (vv. 21-23), this section portrays in the prayer of the prophet the murderous conspiracy of some citizens of his hometown of Anathoth to silence his preaching by assassination. It seemed providential, said Jeremiah, that he discovered the murderous scheme of his compatriots. He was so naive, so trusting, so ready to believe—as an unsuspecting lamb—but to his astonishment he learned of their evil intent. The foul purpose of the conspirators was placed in their mouths (v. 19), an outrage that stirs his righteous indignation. With an appeal to Yahweh of hosts, who is the righteous judge and the evaluator of human thought and motivation, Jeremiah pleaded for vengeance upon such duplicity. Elsewhere in a dialogue with Yahweh the same prayer with its confidence and call for a curse was repeated, all of which permits us to assume the frustration was deeply felt by the prophet (compare 20:12).

The poetic form gives way to prose, where in less impassioned form the plot is again described with the response to Jeremiah's prayer indicated. Here, once again, the discovery of the conspiracy was attributed to Yahweh. It involved the men of Anathoth who were so set against the preaching of Jeremiah that they threatened him with his life if he persisted in his denunciations. It appears that they had made contact with Jeremiah and had delivered the ultimatum to him (v. 21). The reply of Yahweh to the prayer of Jeremiah concerning those who threatened his life was that their lot would be the sword and famine which would in the time of the divine visitation annihilate Anathoth (v. 22). In the savage assaults of the Babylonians, as they zeroed in on Jerusalem, Anathoth with its type of uncompromising nationalism would be dealt with in unrestricted barbarity by the invading soldiers.

The First Confession, Part 2: 12:1-6

The prophet began his complaint with an apologetic confession: he recognized that God was right and that to lodge an accusation against his governance would indeed be wrong. Yet, spurred on by the inequalities he saw, the prophet boldly pleaded his case. The question that vexed his soul was theological: Why does the way of the wicked prosper?/Why do all who are treacherous thrive? (12:6b,c). It was a bold but honest query. In every age men have wondered why God, who is both almighty and righteous, should permit such irregularities to exist in his world.

The problem becomes more complicated when the prophet urged that the wicked not only prosper but gain that prosperity by the furtherance of God: "Thou plantest them, and they take root" (v. 2) and that despite their contrary disaffection: God was near in their mouths but far from their hearts. Hypocrisy and apostasy characterized them, not the ethical virtues that merit reward. Such glaring contradictions the prophet could not withstand. He broke out in indignant prayer against the people commanding—and the two verbs are imperative—that Yahweh execute deserved judgment upon the wicked, separating them from the flock of the righteous as sheep destined to be slaughtered (v. 3b,c; compare Matt. 25:32 ff.). How long, he asked, will the land mourn because of the wickedness of people who blasphemously affirm their skepticism that God would not or could not intervene to rectify the situation?

The prophets particularly assumed a sympathy between man and his environment: wickedness dries up and ruins the land with its vegetation and forests, together with the animals living there. All are victimized by the wicked; the land vomits them out (Lev. 18:25). The contrary reaction is true of the righteous. Jeremiah employed this Hebraic concept to express the profundity of the tragedy the wickedness of the Judeans was imposing upon the land.

Yahweh replied to the bold charge of the prophet. He did not address himself to the problem but to the attitude of the prophet. If Jeremiah fainted now and was weary of it all (symbolized by "racing with men" and "succumbing in a land of peace" [AT, v. 5], that is, his past experiences), what would he do when the going gets really rough (signified by "running with horses" and "enduring the pride,") that is, the rank, tropical, and insufferably hot maze of the Jordan?

To substantiate his words, Yahweh revealed that even the brothers and the house of his father had dealt a treacherous blow to Jeremiah and were in full pursuit after him. Though they spoke fair words they were not to be believed (v. 6; compare 11:18 ff.). The poignancy of this new development, when even his own flesh and blood had turned against him, foreshadowed the ominous woes to attend the prophet in coming days.

The Lament of Yahweh over Judah (12:7-13)

This section devotes itself to four subjects regarding Judah: her abandonment by Yahweh (vv. 7,8b,9a); her rebellion (v. 8); her judgment (vv. 7b,8,9-12); and her *gross national product* (v. 13). Yahweh announced that he had forsaken his house, his heritage, and had given the beloved of his soul into the hands of her enemies (v. 7). The reason for this was that Judah had revolted against Yahweh, had turned upon him as a lion, and roared her antagonism against him (v. 8). Judah had been delivered to the foreign adversaries who like birds of prey would devour her, like wild beasts would consume her. The hostile rulers had destroyed the vineyard of Yahweh (Israel; compare Isa. 5:7). They had made the land desolate, and no one seemed to care (vv. 10 ff.). But behind their hostility and destruction was the directive of Yahweh (v. 12). Judah had such potential, such a favorable opportunity (the sowing of wheat), but in the growth process the harvest produced thorns. The labor went for nothing and to their shame. What else could they expect when their works became evil? It was a *gross* national product, great in its potential, gross in its result.

The Potential of International Weal (12:14-17)

The oracle concerns itself with the evil neighbors who have harassed the land of Israel. Exile is forecast for them while restoration is promised for Judah, upon whom Yahweh would have compassion. The nations, though evil, should they learn the ways of the people of Yahweh and own him as of ultimate significance for life and meaning, would be built up. If, however, they refuse, they would be destroyed.

This oracle of hope is in keeping with Jeremiah's role as a prophet to the nations. It indicates the concern of Yahweh for all people, even evil nations, who have desolated the covenant people. It portrays a marvelous understanding of the role of Israel as a trusted guide of the nations ("the ways of my people") and the resultant attraction of those who made a favorable response.

Admonitions to Judah (13:1-27)

The Pantomime of the Waistcloth (13:1-11)

An enactment of an object lesson was provided when Jeremiah in response to an inner impulse purchased a waistcloth, proceeded to the Euphrates, and hid it in a cleft of the rock (vv. 1-4). Many days later he returned to retrieve the waistcloth only to discover that it was spoiled and worthless (vv. 5-7). The meaning of this action is then given. The worthless waistcloth was Judah, once highly favored of Yahweh as a prized article of apparel, now ruined and worthless— a sorry state brought about by the pride, arrogance, evil, stubbornness and idolatry of Judah. The waistcloth motif is exceedingly bold (v. 11) in that Yahweh anticipated that Israel would be for him a people, a name, a praise, and a glory, that the nations might see in the national life of Judah a reflection of the greatness and goodness of Yahweh; but, alas, the program was ruined by the sin of Judah.

The Parable of the Wine Jar (13:12-14)

The prophet opened with a trite saying which was mockingly turned aside by his audience. "Of course, the wine jars will be filled with wine; that is their purpose!" (v. 12, AT). But, countered the prophet, it will be the wine of judgment wherewith Yahweh will intoxicate the kings, priests, the prophets, and the populace of Jerusalem. In their drunkenness they will destroy one another, even their closest kinfolk, fathers and sons, without mercy or compassion.

A Call to Repentance (13:15-17)

The prophet urged Judah to relinquish her pride and affirm allegiance to Yahweh lest their continued perversity involve them in darkness in which they would surely stumble. Then when they look for light, there will be nothing but gloom and darkness. Sadness for the nation that walked in the darkness is movingly expressed. No doubt, the forlorn hope still flickered in the heart of Jeremiah, but the hour had come for realistic appraisal. Said the prophet, "If you do not listen, my soul will weep in secret for your pride, because captivity awaits the flock of Yahweh" (v. 17, AT).

Oracle to the Royal Family (13:18-19)

A brief word of utmost consequence to the royal family was directed to the king and queen mother who were in immediate danger of exile. From the royal throne they will be debased. Their beautiful royal crowns would be taken from their heads. The stage was all set for such a disaster. The cities of the Negeb (south Palestine) were presently under siege, with no forces to relieve them. Judah would be taken captive and dragged into exile.

A Pathetic Lament over Deplorable Conditions (13:20-27)

The prophet asked Judah to witness the incoming foe from the north and to reflect on the once beautiful flock of Yahweh—the prosperous farms and cities of Judah. What will it all mean? It would be a new government, a foreign power now turned hostile which was once friendly. The national situation would resemble the pain of a woman in travail, with deep searching within her heart. If Judah asked, Why have these things come upon me? the obvious answer was the greatness of her iniquity. It would be such a horrible disaster that the women of Judah would be given away or sold on the market block, shamefully exposed (compare Nah. 3:5). There is no real hope, no possibility of change. If nature can be totally overturned, the Ethiopian can change the color of his skin, and the leopard his spots, then Judah, so accustomed to evil, might then also practice goodness. The judgment will fall, and, like the chaff driven by the wind from the desert, Judah would be scattered abroad. It

was a judgment carefully determined, the order meted out by
Yahweh (vv. 25-27).

Communal Laments (14:1 to 15:9)

In this portion the following elements may be identified: Part 1,
The Lament over the Drought (14:1-6), The People's Penitential
Prayer (14:7-9), The Oracle of Response (14:10-12 f.); Part 2, The
Dialogue with Yahweh Concerning the False Optimism of the
Prophets (14:13-14), The Announcement of Judgment (14:15-18), The
Penitential Supplication of the Laity (14:19-22), The Reiterated
Divine Rejection of Judah (15:1-4), and A Lament of Yahweh over
Jerusalem (15:5-9).

Part 1, The Lament over the Drought (14:1-6)

Droughts were a constant problem in the ancient Near East and
brought untold suffering and death to the areas afflicted. In the
thought of Israel, Yahweh was almighty, and all nature was under his
immediate control. Droughts were interpreted to be the manifesta-
tion of the displeasure of God with the distressed area. Accordingly,
Judah and Jerusalem viewed the drought as a visible evidence of
Yahweh's anger.

The drought and its attendant misery are pathetically described.
The attitude of the nation was one of deepest concern and alarm.
There was no water in the cisterns, no rain upon the land. The
livestock starved in the fields; even the hardy wild asses wasted away
in the wilderness. The people lamented pathetically, with their
heads covered and with a mournful dirge at some sacred spot. Here
it would be, of course, the Temple in Jerusalem.

The People's Penitential Prayer (14:7-9)

The opportunity was not lost to formulate a fitting prayer for the
dire occasion. With a flowery confession of sin, the petition was
presented to Yahweh to act for his name's sake in the perilous
disaster (v. 7). Beginning with the formulas of trust, the prayer
invoked Yahweh as the hope and savior of Israel in time of trouble.
He was asked why he stood off from the disaster as a stranger or
wayfarer with no vested concern or as a man confused or powerless
to help (vv. 8-9a). Such reproachful questions are regularly found in

the psalms of lament (compare Pss. 22:1; 44:24; 74:1,10). The lament ends with an appeal to Yahweh, who was in the midst of his people and by whose name the petitioners were called, not to forsake them (v. 9*b*).

The Oracle of Response (14:10-12)

As in the normal penitential composition, God responded to the prayer of the people. This response assumes the form of an oracle and is interlaced with the various formulas of the prayer. Here Yahweh rejected the prayer. The prophet, here the spokesman of Yahweh, declared that the disobedient people with their unrestrained permissiveness were unacceptable. Their sin and iniquity prevailed over their insincere repentance and would bring calamity upon them. Moreover, the prophet was told no longer to pray for the people, for Yahweh was determined to consume them by war and natural disaster, despite their multiplied rituals (compare 6:20). It must be added that there is always an historical contingency in the prophetic dooms. The judgment is directed in a temporal situation against a particular immoral condition; if, however, the latter is modified and improved, by the same degree the judgment will be moderated. It might seem heartless for Yahweh to reject such a pathetic prayer as 14:7-9 and to disregard the lament of the distressed Judeans in 14:1-6, but their petitions were hardly born of authentic repentance despite their moving eloquence.

Part 2, The Dialogue with Yahweh Concerning the False Optimism of the Prophets (14:13-14)

Jeremiah noticed the optimism of the prophets before Yahweh. They assured the people that there would be no war, no disaster, but glorious peace in their days. They appealed to the popular wishes and were readily accepted as they assured the people that what they wanted would indeed be theirs. Yahweh responded by disowning them entirely: he did not send (commission) them, nor command them to go, nor did he speak to them. What they were prophesying was a lying vision of their own fantasy, empty conjurings, and delusive projections.

The Announcement of Judgment (14:15-18)

Such self-appointed prophets, so misinformed and deluded, would indeed meet the fateful day they had rejected with its stern judgment of famine and war in all its brutality for the entire people no less than their own immediate families (vv. 15-16). Then Yahweh told Jeremiah to add this word (vv. 17-18). It is not vindictiveness. There is no sadism in the motivation of the judgment. There is nothing but sorrow that the religious community had so led the people astray. In a passionate lament, the prophet longed for unceasing tears for the very grievous wound of the virgin daughter of Israel. He then specified what he meant by the medical symbol: it was war, famine, and plague, both in the country and in the city. And the worst of the matter was that these empty-headed prophets and priests practiced their trade briskly throughout the land, only aggravating the coming disaster (vv. 18 ff.).

The Penitential Supplication of the Laity (14:19-22)

The appropriate rejection of the people by Yahweh gave rise to a protest formulated in three questions: Have you (Yahweh) utterly rejected Judah? Why does your soul (seemingly) loathe Zion? Is there no healing in your judgment? Questions such as these are often encountered in communal laments. The composition then describes the disappointment of the people as they looked for peace and healing but no good came, nothing but terror (v. 19). A confession of sin followed and was succeeded by a prayer that they be not spurned and that Yahweh remember his covenant, a prayer motivated by the honor of Yahweh's name (v. 20 ff.). The lament concludes with an affirmation of faith. After an acknowledgment that the false gods could not give rain—an implication that these false gods are no answer to the problem—the people asserted that their hope was in Yahweh who alone controls nature.

The Reiterated Divine Rejection of Judah (15:1-4)

Despite the eloquence and insistence of the people's pleas Yahweh was adamant in his purpose to judge the nation. Were the most notable intercessors of the past, Moses and Samuel, to plead the Judean cause it would avail nothing. The Exile was a determined appointment with all its frightful and tragic, heartrending suffering: pestilence, war, famine, and exile. This is the horrible end, the terminal point of the vile years of King Manasseh, a period of untold orgies and wickedness, a period hardly improved upon by the contemporary kings and people.

It should be remembered that the dire doom of Judah might have been changed had the people truly changed their ways. But in actual fact they did not. Consequently, the only method left to Yahweh was to thrust them into the cleansing of the Exile. History testifies that it was out of that painful schooling that a new nation with changed life and purpose was born, and the historical destiny of Israel was thereby preserved for the blessing of mankind.

A Lament of Yahweh over Jerusalem (15:5-9)

The tragic situation of Jerusalem with all her delinquent ways—which would occasion her end without mourners as one forsaken and alone—brought from the heart of Yahweh this moving lament. In three rhetorical questions addressed to Jerusalem he inquired if any would pity or bemoan or inquire for Jerusalem. The answer need not be expressed; it is so obvious: No one! (v. 5). Yahweh then listed the reasons for the deserved judgment. The nation had rejected him, ever departing farther from his ways. Disciplinary measures proved unavailing; his patience had now come to an end (v. 6). Nevertheless he would review the ineffective dealings he had with Judah before now. He had winnowed them in their gates, bereaved and destroyed the people, but they refused to be moved or to turn from their evil practices. Widows were multiplied and eligible mothers destroyed in the unsettled, belligerent times. Anguish and terror suddenly swooped down upon them. The mother of seven swooned as her sons were forcefully taken away. They were as ashamed as a woman whose reproach (childlessness) had not been removed by pregnancy. And those that did not fit into those categories perished with the sword (vv. 7-9).

The Second Confession of Jeremiah (15:10-21)

A Personal Woe of Jeremiah (15:10-14)

In a self-pitying vein the prophet lamented his fate. Though he had neither lent nor borrowed, which might have given rise to such reaction, all men curse him. He deplored the fact that his mother bore a son who had become the bitter object of strife to the whole of the land (v. 10; compare Job 3). What follows is ambiguous. As it stands in the Revised Standard Version, the prophet continued with a curse to the effect that if he has not had the good of the nation at heart, if he has not entreated Yahweh for his enemies in their hour of trial and trouble, may his personal problems then continue (v. 11). On the other hand, the two verses (vv. 11-12) may be an independent fragment describing the destruction of the invading foe and thus indicating the exile of the Judeans. It would then be translated thus:

> Yahweh said, "Surely I have made an enemy [Babylon] for you [Judah] for good. In a time of evil and in a time of distress will one [you] break iron, iron from the north, [the enemy] and bronze? Your wealth and your treasures I will give as spoil, without price, for all your sins, throughout all your territory. I will make you serve your enemies in a land which you do not know, for in my anger a fire is kindled which shall burn forever (AT, vv. 11-14).

The resultant meaning would be that the foes of Judah are irresistible and enduring and have been so appointed by Yahweh (v. 11). No defense can be mustered against the northern foe. It will despoil the nation of its wealth, and that for its sins; and exile will be its lot. The same prediction is partially restated in 17:3-4.

The Second Confession of Jeremiah (15:15-18)

This Confession begins with an urgent plea for Yahweh to take vengeance on the enemies of Jeremiah. There follows a picture of the suffering of the prophet for Yahweh's cause. He does not wish death but would remind Yahweh that it was for his sake that he is bearing reproach (v. 15). He related how he had received the message and his consecration from Yahweh with joy, that he had shunned the merry crowd to dedicate himself with a monastic zeal to his task (vv. 16 ff.); but within that experience there arose anxiety and doubt: Would his suffering be perpetual? Would Yahweh prove undependable? (v. 18). Hard thoughts, but honest, born from a momentary lapse in the perception of faith.

The Response of Yahweh (15:19-21)

Yahweh gently chided the prophet for his undue pessimism and for his nearsighted inability to perceive the ultimate good. Not less commitment, but more was demanded—less self-pity and more confidence in Yahweh's personal commitment to him. Yahweh urged him to return and be restored, to stand again before him (the role of a servant), to separate the precious from the worthless and thus become more truly the divine messenger. There was to be no compromise with the people. The terms of salvation were inflexible:

a repentance of life and correction of their ways. In this rededication the prophet should be assured of complete adequacy, despite the attacks of the people, a sufficiency earlier granted in his inaugural call (1:20 ff.) and emphatically repeated here. The foe was formidable, wicked, and ruthless. There would certainly be ugly fighting, but the prophet was strengthened with an overcoming power against overwhelming odds and would experience the presence of Yahweh as a comrade in arms in the deadly struggle (vv. 20-21).

The Fearful Doom of Judah (16:1-13)

The verses may be divided according to their topics as follows: (1) The Sign of the Celibate (vv. 1-4); (2) Fraternity Prohibited (vv. 5-9); and (3) Disaster and Its Justification (vv. 10-13).

The Sign of the Celibate (16:1-4)

The prophet was forbidden to marry and to have children because the people—sons, daughters, mothers, fathers—are doomed to die, whether by sword or famine or plague occasioned by the coming Babylonian invasion. Such care to produce a family and such a futile, tragic end to it all is reason enough to dissuade the prophet from this heartache.

Marriages are sometimes discouraged so that an undivided commitment may be given to the Kingdom. Unusual situations demand unusual sacrifice. Marriage and the family are normal in the divine plan (Gen. 1:28), and the truth still stands that it is not good that man should be alone (Gen. 2:18). In the Old Testament some aspects of marriage are illustrative of the prophetic message. In the case of Jeremiah, his celibacy illustrated the chaotic future through which the nation was to pass, a time hardly suited for family life.

Fraternity Prohibited (16:5-9)

The prophet was commanded to enter neither the house of mourning nor the house of feasting. In the former injunction he was to indicate by his absence that in the day of disaster there will be no one to perform the normal funeral rites or to attend them (compare 9:22). In the latter, the action suggests that no longer will there be gatherings such as joyful matrimonial events. By his unnatural absence from these gatherings he will provide an object lesson to

enforce his message of doom that soon there will be no assembling of
any kind; the people simply will be gone.

One should notice the rituals for the dead: lamentation, the
cutting of oneself, and the shaving of one's head. The latter two
customs were current in the time of Jeremiah, even though they
were prohibited by law.

Disaster and Its Justification (16:10-13)

This question-answer procedure regarding the plundering of Judah is a recurrent literary device in the Old Testament. The prophet
was instructed to reply that the evil is forthcoming because Judah
had forsaken Yahweh for other gods, had failed to keep the law, had
exceeded the evil of their fathers, and had followed stubbornly their
evil will to a man. Accordingly, the indictment firmly demands the
judgment of the Exile with all its accompanying woes.

The New Exodus (16:14-15)

Interrupting the consistent pattern of doom, this oracle has an
entirely different posture and proceeds from a different time. It
comes from the Babylonian Exile, since Yahweh promised to bring
them back to their own land. It portrays a hope for the future
beyond the tragedy of the Exile. In true prophetic style, Yahweh
predicted that in the coming days no longer will the time-honored
oath be phrased, "As [Yahweh] lives who brought up the people of
Israel out of the land of Egypt" (v. 14, AT), but it will be changed to
these words: "As [Yahweh] lives who brought up the people of Israel
out of the north country and out of all the countries where he had
driven them" (v. 15, AT). One swore by the most unchangeable and
transcendent being: the life of God. The oath was then affirmed to
be as established as the entity by which the man swore. In effect, it
was to say, "My word is as certain and guaranteed as the life
(existence) of God." The oath invoked a second undeniable reality:
Yahweh had brought up the Israelites out of the land of Egypt. That
historic Exodus was as rock-ribbed a reality as the very life of God.
And by the truth of the life of God and the absolute certainty of
Yahweh's emancipation of Israel from Egypt the Israelites swore. It
was the ultimate, transcendent reality, and men acknowledged it in
their oaths, as we do the Bible. The new oath coupled the life of

Yahweh with the certainty of a second exodus, that from the Diaspora, and the restoration to the homeland. No greater assurance could be given the troubled Judeans, either in war-torn Judah or in exile, than the newly-formulated oath. It asserted in effect two unchanging truths: Yahweh lives, and the Diaspora will be restored. The latter is as true as the former. Both are in the new oath, and both influence the new mood of the people.

The Thoroughgoing Judgment (16:16-18)

Yahweh will not rest until all who are guilty are involved in the judgment. There will be no escapees in that day. He will summon his prosecutors, the invading foe, to act like fishermen and hunters to find those who have hidden. One can feel the intense hatred of the prophet for the "carcasses [nonentities, corpses] of their detestable idols" (v. 18) and the related abominations which filled the inheritance of Yahweh.

The Conversion of the Nations (16:19-21)

In the form of a prayer the prophet addressed Yahweh as his inward strength and protector, his refuge in the day of trouble. Then in that optimistic mood he prophesied that the nations shall come to Yahweh from the ends of the earth and frankly confess their former religion to be false and profitless. What they and their forebears had made were not gods. They were nothing but lies. Yahweh meets the nations in their powerlessness and humility and promises to make them know his power and his might, and they shall know that his name is Yahweh. It is the saving address of Yahweh to a repentant world. What the world could be if it but knew Yahweh!

Miscellanea (17:1-13)

The End of a Permissive Generation (17:1-4)

The stubbornness of the sin of Judah is the subject of this divine oracle of doom. Like an inscription written in the rock with an engraver's tool, like a tablet written with the point of a diamond, so Judah's sin is written both in the national life and in her religious disobediences. They have spawned a new generation entirely devoted to the nature cults and busily practicing them everywhere. But judgment will come when the wealth and treasures will be given as a spoil to their enemies because of sin. They will lose their land and serve their enemies in exile, for, says Yahweh, "In my anger a fire is kindled which shall burn for ever."

A Wisdom Psalm (17:5-8)

The psalm is typical of wisdom compositions depicting the two ways confronting men for decision. Its close similarity to Psalm 1 is immediately apparent. In the Jeremianic psalm, a thoroughgoing humanist is compared with one whose trust is in Yahweh. The humanist is viewed as cursed and is likened unto a desert shrub with a bleak future in its inhospitable habitat. On the other hand, the man who trusts in Yahweh is pronounced blessed. He is likened to a tree planted by the streams of water, whose roots reach out to the stream for nourishment, whose leaves remain green when the heat comes, and, even when drought strikes the land, does not cease to bear fruit.

The Heart: Human and Divine (17:9-10)

At times in the Book of Jeremiah there are statements of the greatest importance, insights into human nature among the choicest ever uttered. In this selection, self-knowledge, a popular concern of modern man, is discussed. In declaring that the heart is deceitful above all things and desperately corrupt and unfathomable, Jeremiah was not referring to the heart of the evil man but to the human heart generally. In Hebrew psychology, the heart plays the predominant role in the mental life (compare Prov. 23:7). In verse 10, Yahweh is said to search the heart and the kidneys (KJV, "reins"). The kidneys, situated deep within the body cavity, represent for the Hebrew the deepest component of human personality. Accordingly, the two terms, heart and reins, are roughly equivalent to the modern concept of mind, personality, psyche. The prophet declared that the personality is deceitful above all things. It weaves an illusory spell of self-deception, distortion, and disorientation. Thus we cannot judge ourselves rightly. But in the crucible of God's judgment our proud professions wither and our idolatrous (egotistical) motivations come to light. Yet, affirmed the prophet, though the heart's mysterious intricacies elude and delude us, Yahweh searches (note present tense) and tries the heart of man. The test is of the total person and his life, quantity and quality. The flawless results of the divine test are then awarded to the individual as the fruit of his ways (v. 10).

This thought-provoking section presents a living challenge to the worshiper of Yahweh. There can be no sham, no hypocrisy, no secretiveness in one's relationship to Yahweh. It must be an openhearted, frank, and honest encounter. What man cannot know about himself, his own idiosyncracies, his self-delusions, his too high or too low self-esteem are disclosed in the divine test. In the one-to-one fellowship, information concerning and power to overcome personal defects are provided, and in the end the improved personality is rewarded accordingly.

A Proverb (17:11)

The form of this proverb is emblematic: "Like the partridge that gathers a brood which she did not hatch [the emblem], so is he who gets riches but not by right [the comparison]." Such an unrighteous acquirer will lose his ill-gotten gain in the midst of his years, and at his end he will be a fool (ultimate tragedy). This proverb has little reference to its context unless it is coined to describe King Jehoiakim (compare 22:13-19).

Yahweh, the Hope of Israel (17:12-13)

Hope and admonition are equally represented in this expression. If the words "O [Yahweh], the hope of Israel" are considered the essential affirmation, then verse 12 supports this sentiment by referring to the high privilege Israel has enjoyed from the beginning: the presence of King Yahweh in its midst, present sacramentally in the sanctuary (compare Ps. 80:1). Moreover, the hope of Israel is Yahweh, the fountain of living water (compare 2:13). This is the positive declaration, feelingly uttered. But there is the negative side, the admonition and warning. Those that forsake Yahweh shall be put to shame. They shall be written in the earth, soon erased, soon forgotten.

The Third Confession (17:14-18)

The literary form is that of an individual lament beginning with a prayer to be healed and saved, a petition urged upon Yahweh by the motivating clause: "for thou art my praise," an appeal to the self-interest of Yahweh. The prophet was not physically ill. Rather he was using the terms "heal" and "save" psychosomatically to express the mental and moral torment suffered in his troublesome task.

The description of distress next follows in which the punch lines of his enemies appear: "Where is the word of [Yahweh]? Let it come!" Such an insolent challenge of the divine, profoundly agnostic in its denial, was a complete repudiation of Jeremiah and his mission. It must have cut him to the quick to hear such blasphemy directed not merely against him but against Yahweh. Their words contradict entirely the essential structure of his mission, a mission of love and concern. He had not pressed for their judgment nor had he desired the day of woe. Yahweh was his witness (v. 16).

The confession or, more properly the lament, concludes with a prayer for himself. He prayed that Yahweh would not be a terror to him but rather a refuge in the day of judgment when the world would make little sense. Jeremiah then called for a curse on his enemies as those that stand in the way of everything good, true, and desirable. Let them be ashamed, not me; let them be dismayed, not me; bring on them the evil day and double destruction (vv. 17 ff.).

The Keeping of the Sabbath (17:19-27)

The writing style of this section is prose. Some argue that the ideas that the keeping of the sabbath and the studious maintenance of the sacrificial cult would be a cure-all for Judah are quite uncharacteristic of the basic pattern of Jeremianic thought. Jeremiah's usual emphasis falls on the inner and spiritual aspects of religion, not in the externals.

Yahweh commanded Jeremiah to publish in the gates of Jerusalem to the great and small a word concerning the sabbath commandment. The Fourth Commandment had been flaunted. If continued, this practice would spell the doom of Jerusalem. On the other hand, if the people observed the sabbath, the nation would abide continually and offerings would be brought into the house of Yahweh from all over Judah. This seems a rather simplistic view and hardly accords with the deeper complexion of the moral life of the nation nor with Jeremiah's insistence on religion as an inner, personal experience of the heart. The entire tone of this section is more in keeping with the later legalism of the Exilic and post-Exilic periods.

The Pantomime of the Potter's Vessel (18:1-12)

Directed by Yahweh, the prophet visited the potter's shop as he was working at his wheel. The clay vessel on which the potter was working was spoiled. Undaunted, the potter reworked the clay into another vessel (vv. 1-4). Jeremiah perceived in this experience a symbol of the divine workings. Like clay in the potter's hand, so Judah is in the hand of Yahweh. If evil prevails in a nation and Yahweh determines to punish that people, repentance and correction of life can change the original design into a new form, that of stability and well-being. On the contrary, if the original program of Yahweh was constructive and the nation fell into an evil pattern, the new formulation of the divine purpose would change to one of woe and destruction (compare Ezek. 18). The appropriateness of the allegory here is that Judah now is evil, and the purposes of Yahweh accord with that situation; but should the nation repent, the intent of Yahweh would change accordingly, from evil into blessing. It is an invitation to repent and thus avoid the coming disaster presently programmed by the nation's sin.

The prophet then reported the sad verdict of the witless people: "That is utopianism, impractical, vanity. We will proceed with our own plans and will adhere consistently to the dictates of our best thinkers" (author's paraphrase, v. 12). The people would hardly have judged their words as dictated by "the stubbornness of [an] evil heart." That moral judgment was supplied by the prophet (v. 12).

An Oracle of Doom (18:13-17)

The oracle begins with three questions: Have the nations ever heard the like? Does the snow of Lebanon vanish? Do the mountain streams run dry? After the first question is the parenthetic announcement that the virgin Israel has done a horrible, an unheard-of thing. The three questions are to be firmly answered in the

negative. No, such matters do not occur. What a sorry contrast to
these unchangeable, enduring, and perennial actualities is the
fickle, erratic, and inconstant behavior of the people of Yahweh!
They have forgotten Yahweh, burned incense to false gods, and have
consequently stumbled. Thus in untrodden paths, forsaking the old
ways, the ancient and tried road, they have caused the ruin of their
land. It is a horror to all who pass by. The oracle ends with the
fearful prediction that the people of Judah will be scattered before
the enemy with the violence of an east wind. They will not have a
face-to-face experience with their God. Rather, he will turn his back
on them, as they have done to him.

The Fourth Confession (18:18-23)

Plots Against Jeremiah (18:18)

Whether or not this verse follows from the preceding oracle of
doom is an open question, but the substance of the saying is a
verbatim recital of the threats of his enemies. The gist of the plot is
that the conspirators are fully confident in their religious advisers:
priests, wise men, and prophets. Their teaching, counsel, and
advice give light on all possibilities and stop all national dangers.
This then is their full persuasion; but what can be done to the
persistent, irritating voice of the prophet Jeremiah, who contradicts
the advice of our mentors, weakens public morale, and divides the
nation? One thing is certain: we shall never follow his lead; rather
we shall smite him with the tongue and plot his professional
downfall. The nation is not large enough to have two voices in Judah.
One must go; and we are firmly persuaded that Jeremiah must
somehow be discredited and silenced once and for all.

The Fourth Confession (18:19-23)

Again it may be asked whether the preceding verse gave rise to
this fourth lament or not. The composition opens with a brief prayer
and immediately plunges into the description of distress. My
enemies have returned evil for good. They have dug a pit for my life,
and that despite the fact that I interceded with you, Yahweh, for
their good, to turn your wrath from them (v. 20). Then follows an
intense prayer in which the prophet gave vent to his pent-up anger.
In petition after petition he urged Yahweh to destroy his enemies

because they have unrighteously plotted his death.

The imprecatory prayers of Jeremiah and of the Book of Psalms generally petition the universal Lord to a course of action which a Christian conscience deplores. Jeremiah asked Yahweh to give his enemies' children to famine and to the power of the sword, the wives of his foes to childlessness and widowhood, the men to pestilence, and their youth to be slain in battle (v. 21). Moreover, he prayed that an outcry from their houses may be heard as the marauder breaks in suddenly upon them with fury (v. 22). The prophet appears willing to have many sacrificed—and granted they are evil—in order that he might be preserved (compare 18:18). The Christian ethic instructs its followers to love their enemies and pray for those who persecute them.

Desecration, Execration, Ruination (19:1-13)

The chapter may be divided into three parts: the doom pronounced upon Judah by Jeremiah in the valley of Topheth (vv. 1-9); the execration ritual consisting in the breaking of a potter's vessel as the symbol of the coming doom (vv. 10-13); and the reiteration of the judgment in the Temple (vv. 14-15). Execration rites or ceremonies associated with cursing were common in the ancient Near East and are here and there in the literature of the Old Testament.

The Desecration (19:1-9)

The oracle begins with a command to the prophet to get a potter's earthen flask, to take a few elders and senior priests as witnesses, and to proceed to the valley of the son of Hinnom. There Jeremiah solemnly charged the people with their monstrous sins; they had forsaken Yahweh, burned incense to other gods, filled the land with the blood of innocents, and burned their sons as offerings to Baal, an abomination unthinkable and alien to all Yahweh had said (vv. 1-5). Notice how often Jeremiah ranks first the abandonment of God and then the resultant evil practices.

The prophet now pronounced the curses. The valley shall no longer be called Topheth, or the valley of the son of Hinnom (located on the south side of Jerusalem), but the valley of Slaughter. There the plans of Judah will be thwarted, and there the people will perish before their enemies, the multiplied corpses left unburied, carrion for the beastly scavengers. The complete destruction of the city will cause all who pass it in the future to be horrified. It will be known for its bloody slaughter and cannibalism in its last hours (vv. 6-9).

The Execration Ritual (19:10-13)

Then the prophet proceeded to break the flask and utter the curse: "So will I break this people as one breaks a potter's vessel, so that it can never be mended." The basic idea is that of sympathetic magic: what happens to the jar will occur to the city by means of the ritual and the curse. The toll of the death is prophesied to be so many that even Topheth with its eerie associations will be used as a burial place. Indeed, the entire city of Jerusalem will be like a valley of Slaughter with the houses of Jerusalem and the kings of Judah desecrated like Topheth because of their devotion to astral and foreign gods. If Israel's conception of God was radically false, then the more devout she was the worse it became for her.

The Sequel to Topheth (19:14 to 20:6)

The Announcement of Doom (19:14-15)

Jeremiah returned from his announcement of doom in the valley of Topheth and gave the gist of his message to the people assembled in the court of Yahweh's house. The reason for the announced doom was Judah's refusal to obey the word of Yahweh (19:14-15).

Jeremiah's Confrontation with Pashhur (20:1-6)

Among the crowd in the court of Yahweh's house was Pashhur, the priest and chief officer of the Temple. He ordered Jeremiah seized and beaten, then placed in stocks in the upper Benjamin Gate of the Temple (vv. 1 ff.). When Jeremiah was released the following day, he encountered Pashhur with indignation and forecast that Pashhur would be dubbed with a new name, "Terror on every side," a terror both to himself and to his friends as they were slain by the invaders. All of Judah, prophesied Jeremiah, would be delivered into the hands of the Babylonian king together with its wealth and prized treasures, which would be transported to Babylon. Moreover, Pashhur and his house would likewise be taken into captivity and would die in exile. Then his friends would discover the falsity of his optimistic policies. The tragedy of such a misguided cleric is that he involved his unquestioning followers in his disastrous ways.

Jeremiah's Fifth Confession (20:7-13)

The pathetic lament begins with a reproach (compare Ps. 22:1). Yahweh, said the prophet, had deceived him; he felt let down. When he asserted that Yahweh is stronger than he and had prevailed, does he mean that Yahweh has vanquished him with argument and that he had finally succumbed? In that case verse 7*c,d* would refer immediately to verse 7*a,b*. But it seems more to the point to believe that Jeremiah accused Yahweh of using his great power, his strength, his overwhelming might to overpower him. It is an unequal struggle that causes the prophet to lose credibility. He had become laughable in the eyes of his contemporaries. Everyone mocked him. And yet he had adopted this course of life and uttered this word of doom for Yahweh's sake. When he cried, "Violence and destruction!" he was written off with ridicule. Overwhelmed by Yahweh and mocked by the Judeans into silence, Jeremiah faced a deep dilemma: if he refused to speak, the resultant spiritual state was worse than suffering the stinging criticism of the people when he did speak. To refuse the burden (cross) of Yahweh confined within him a burning fire, shut up in his bones. He was wearied with holding it in; indeed, he could not! Yet he heard the whispering, the terror, the destructive words of his former friends: "Denounce him . . . perhaps he will overstep; then we can prevail and take our revenge upon him" (v. 10, AT). Despite the harshness of the hour and the spiritual struggle within, Jeremiah fought through the despair till he became assured that the battle was Yahweh's who as a dread warrior would overcome his foes with shame and dishonor (v. 11). At that plateau of assurance Jeremiah prayed to Yahweh who knows all, who tries the righteous, and perceives the heart and the mind, that Jeremiah may see vengeance upon his adversaries because he had committed his cause wholly to Yahweh. In this struggle, the prophet gained a confidence, and the confidence brought a joy that his prayer had been heard and the answer may fittingly be anticipated in praise (v. 13). It is a call beyond the tragedy of the moment to sing to Yahweh, to which the prophet added the justifiable reason that God delivers the life of the needy from the hand of evildoers.

This confession is one of the most intense we have thus far encountered. It pictures the servant of Yahweh suffering for the sake of God as he ministers to a thankless, thoughtless people unaware of

what was tragically transpiring. It is the suffering servant bearing
stripes and wounds that others might be healed.

Jeremiah's Sixth Confession (20:14-18)

One can see in the life of Jeremiah, as in the life of all truly great
men, the flood tide of confidence and the ebb tide of despair. It is
the latter we now encounter. The prophet lamented that he was ever
conceived; or, being conceived, was not stillborn. He will not curse
Yahweh in blasphemy, but he approximates such when he cursed the
day his mother bore him. Not merely the day should be cursed, but
the messenger that brought the joyful news to his father (compare
2 Sam. 18:19-28; Job 3). May that man be like Sodom and Gomorrah
(v. 16); may alarm disturb him ever because he did not kill me in the
womb as a stillborn. His lament ends with the poignant question,
"Why did I come forth from the womb to see toil and sorrow, and
spend my days in shame?" (v. 18).

At first we are repelled by the self-pitying pessimism of the
lament, but there are important arguments to urge that here is one
of the masterpieces of religious experience. In the first place, it is
honest-to-God religion. He was telling it as it is; it was not
counterfeited, feigned, or misrepresented. However painful it is, his
words are true, unadulterated, and sincere. Second, it was his own
personal experience. Whatever others may feel matters little at this
point; it was his own perception. Third, the great religious personalities have all shared in darkness, gloom, and pessimistic experiences. Job expresses the wish never to have been and for speedy
annihilation (ch. 3). Even Jesus had moments of deepest sorrow
(John 13:21; Matt. 27:46; Heb. 5:7). It is an integral part of life and
not to be lightly criticized. And, finally, crossbearing, suffering for
God's sake, depression, and pessimism are areas of healing, to afford
time to determine what is and what is not essential, to separate the
trivial from the meaningful, the evil from the good (compare 15:19c).
To appreciate light fully we must know darkness; to cherish health
totally we must experience illness; to gain spiritual triumph and
victorious living we must pass through the difficult, the unhappy,
and the undesired. Nothing will replace the negative as a challenge.
If rightly used, its teaching produces the highest education. The
profoundest moment of Christ's suffering was on the cross; it was also
his highest glory, the center round which the Christian revolves.

Prophecies of Jeremiah Largely After Jehoiakim
21:1 to 25:38

Jeremiah and the Babylonian Siege (21:1-14)

The chapter is logically divided into four parts: The Mission of Zedekiah (vv. 1-2); The Response of Jeremiah (vv. 3-7); The Report of the People (vv. 8-10); and the Moral Exhortation to the Royal House (vv. 11-12). The chapter ends with an oracle of doom (vv. 13-14).

The Mission of Zedekiah (21:1-2)

When the Babylonians were besieging Jerusalem sometime in late 589 or early 588 BC, Zedekiah sent an embassy to Jeremiah composed of Pashhur the son of Malchiah and Zephaniah the son of Maaseiah asking him to inquire of Yahweh as to the outcome of the struggle with Nebuchadnezzar, slyly suggesting that the prophet intervene with Yahweh to deal with Jerusalem according to all his marvelous deeds (miraculously) and to cause Nebuchadnezzar to withdraw from the city (vv. 1-2).

The Response of Jeremiah (21:3-7)

Jeremiah responded to the query with the affirmation that the weapons of Judah would be utterly ineffective and that Yahweh would fight against the city himself. Pestilence, famine, and the sword would deliver Judah into the hands of the Babylonians who would ravage the populace (vv. 3-7).

The Report of the People (21:8-10)

The prophet addressed himself to the people in the surrounded city and forecast a picture of gloom. They could fight on only to perish miserably; or they could surrender to the Babylonians, the better of the alternatives. One thing was certain in Jeremiah's mind: Yahweh would deliver Jerusalem into the Babylonian power and the city would be burned by the foe (vv. 8-10).

Moral Exhortation to the Royal House (21:11-12)

A further oracle was given the royal house by Jeremiah: it is an injunction to stay even now the divine wrath by moral reformation—

to execute justice speedily and to deliver the oppressed (compare 22:3; vv. 11-12).

An Oracle of Doom (21:13-14)

The oracle of doom which concludes the chapter takes its theme from the final threatening words to the royal house. The wrath of Yahweh is described as a confrontation of Yahweh against Jerusalem. He is depicted as enthroned above the valley and the rocky plateau whose dwellers boast that they are invincible (v. 13). Yahweh assured the highly complacent inhabitants that he would punish them for their doings (v. 14).

Counsel to the Davidic House (22:1-30)

Admonition to the Judean Monarch (22:1-10)

The royal house was addressed, together with the nation at large and urged to become a righteous society. The theme, having been suggested in verse 11, is here restated more fully. It embraces justice and righteousness, the deliverance from oppression due to robbery, treating the alien residents equitably, protecting the socially dispossessed, and avoiding shedding the blood of the innocent (v. 3). If such morality results, the monarchy would persist. If not, it would become a desolation (v. 5 ff.). The latter alternative is then reinforced by two oracles: the first in poetry, the second in prose. The first indicates the bravery of Judah, comparing it with the richness of Gilead and the eminence of Lebanon. Yet if the nation morally defects, it will become as a desert, an uninhabited city (v. 6). Yahweh would prepare destroyers and, with Lebanon as the picture, will see that the choicest cedars are felled and burned (v. 7), an allegorical portrait of the doom of Judah. The second oracle casts its imagery in the conversation of the nations who have occasion to pass by the ruined city and inquire as to the cause of the disaster. The immediate answer is returned: the city forsook the covenant of their God and worshiped and served other gods; wherefore Yahweh has dealt thus with it (vv. 8-9; compare for this picture 5:19; 13:22; 16:10-11; Deut. 29:24 ff.; 1 Kings 9:8 f.).

A Lament over Jehoahaz (Shallum) (22:11-12)

The pitiful ending of Jehoahaz, here referred to by his popular name Shallum, is given in 2 Kings 23:31-34 (compare 2 Chron.

35:20-24). When the Egyptian pharaoh had slain Josiah at Megiddo in 609 BC, the Judeans placed Jehoahaz, his son, on the throne; but after a brief reign of three months, Neco put him in bonds at Riblah in the land of Hamath and transported him to Egypt. The lament asks the people not to weep for Josiah, who had been killed in battle, but rather for Jehoahaz who had been taken captive to Egypt, for he would die there and never again see his native land (vv. 11 ff.).

A Denunciation Against Jehoiakim (22:13-19)

Jeremiah uttered a woe against the unrighteous acts of Jehoiakim (609-598 BC), who was placed on the throne by Pharaoh Neco instead of the deposed Jehoahaz. The unscrupulous practices of Jehoiakim in the building of his new palace are here flagrantly exposed. He had breached his contract with his laborers and in a very strained economy had built a showy dwelling, wholly out of keeping with an enlightened ruler. Note the extravagance of his building plans: "A great house with spacious upper rooms," furnished with windows and paneling of cedar and painted bright red. The prophet wryly asked: "Do you think you are a king because you compete in cedar?" Josiah your father did justice and righteousness, and well-being in the nation resulted. He judged the cause of the poor and the needy. This was to know Yahweh and to fulfill the responsibilities and privileges of a king; but you, Jehoiakim, have no eyes and no heart save for dishonest gain, for shedding innocent blood, for practicing oppression and violence. It was a stern, bold denunciation of an arrogant and ruthless king. The tirade concludes with this formidable oracle: there will be no one to lament your death; it will be regarded as a funeral unclean and repulsive.

An Announcement of Doom (22:20-23)

Judah was bidden to give vent to her sorrow that her lovers (political allies) were destroyed and to voice the disappointment from the highest elevations in Palestine: Lebanon, Bashan, and Abarim in Moab. Though Yahweh had foretold the disastrous results, and that despite the national prosperity, Judah remained unconvinced. She refused to bow to Yahweh's command, a posture persistent from the nation's very beginning. There follows the renewed description of the impotence of the allies of Judah: the wind will drive them aimlessly and ultimately into captivity. Judah will then be ashamed of her wickedness. Now like the proud inhabitant of Lebanon, she will be debased and groan as a woman in travail as she stands alone, and racked with pain.

An Oracle to Jehoiachin (22:24-27)

There are two oracles—one in prose, the other in poetry—concerned with Jehoiachin (Coniah), the successor to Jehoiakim, who having reigned but three months surrendered on the 16th of March 597 BC to Nebuchadnezzar and was deported to Babylon (52:28). The oracle predicts that though Jehoiachin was the signet ring on the right hand of Yahweh (compare Hag. 2:23), he would be torn off and given into the hands of the Babylonians. The determination of Yahweh to destroy Jerusalem is here adamantly affirmed. Not only will the king go into captivity, but also the royal family, nobles, the state officials, and the leading citizens would be exiled to a strange and alien land and there die.

The Poetic Oracle (22:28-30)

In a rhetorical question it is asked if Jehoiachin is a despised, broken pot, a vessel of concern to no one. The implied answer is no. Why then, continues the speaker, are he and his children exiled into a foreign land? The reply to the question does not appear; it was obvious in the context of historical situation. The oracle concludes with the word of Yahweh stipulating that Jehoiachin would be childless and without successor, having no offspring to sit on the throne of David in Jerusalem (vv. 28-30).

Messianic Hopes (23:1-8)

Woe and Weal (23:1-4)

The woe is delivered against the shepherds (the rulers) who destroy and scatter the sheep of Yahweh's pasture (the Judean nation). Here Jeremiah may have in mind such monarchs as Jehoiakim and Zedekiah, together with their state functionaries. Their policies would ultimately lead the state into ruin at every level; the political, social, economic, and religious strength and unity had disintegrated through their inattention and erring policies. They stand under Yahweh's judgment for their wrongdoing (vv. 1-2).

However, Yahweh will shepherd the remnant of his scattered flock and return them to their homeland, where they will be fruitful and multiply and where Yahweh will set up worthy shepherds (rulers) who will care for them and provide a stable government (vv. 3 ff.; compare 30:3 where the same thought occurs).

Two Messianic Prophecies (23:5-8)

The prophet forecasted that the future would see a son of David ascend the throne of his father and rule with justice and righteousness. In his day both Judah and Israel will be saved from their disastrous situation and will enjoy security. The king will bear a name symbolic of his reign; he will be called "[Yahweh] is our righteousness" (v. 6; compare 33:14 where the verses are repeated amid a cluster of messianic predictions).

The second messianic oracle predicts the return of the scattered people of Israel to their own land. It is forcefully announced as the oath that men will take when solemnly contracting a matter. The former formula of swearing will be replaced by the new oath. This makes the regathering of the dispersed Israel an event of sacred certainty (vv. 7-8). The date of the prophecy appears to be exilic.

The messianic hope centralized in the descendant of David the mission originally given to father Abraham (Gen. 12:1-3), then nationalized in the covenant at Sinai (Ex. 19:5 ff.). The nucleus of the nation, when it assumed the monarchical form, was the king. In a real sense through the idea of corporate personality, the king was the nation, and the nation was the king. In verse 5 and following (compare 33:15 ff.), it is not clear whether the author had in mind one king or the dynasty. Whether the two nations Judah and Israel are to be conceived as reunited under a Davidic monarch and whether the hopes expressed are ideally viewed and assume some objectivity merely to convey some structure for the fulfillment of the messianic hope remain open questions. It would certainly appear that Jeremiah viewed these prophecies as predicting the restoration of the Davidic throne after the Exile and the union of Judah and Israel as one nation. Like other prophecies that were unfulfilled, some historical contingency intervened. Probably the forecast was fulfilled in the Suffering Servant (Isa. 53), in whose ministry dynasty and nationalism disappeared and the universal dimensions of the gospel resulted. In the view of the Christian the prophecy was fulfilled in the large dimension of the Christian mission.

An analogy may be helpful in attempting to understand what the prophet was attempting to convey in these messianic words. Suppose we view him as one who lived in the medieval period, say, AD

800. He wished to say something to the twentieth century, to convey the precious thought of his day to our day. He certainly did not know the modern scientific world in which we live; but he had at his disposal various objects such as the Davidic king and dynasty, the reunion of Israel, the blessing of the world (compare 3:15-18; 4:2), and other messianic benefits. In these terms he prophesied. His views were incomplete as literal predictions but complete when interpreted as fulfilled, not in a Davidic king, but in King Jesus; not in the union of two small Near Eastern countries, but in the universal people of Yahweh, the church of God; not in absorbing the Gentiles into the nationalism of Israel, but in a world society wherein Jew and Gentile cannot and do not exist; and where the blessings are not materialistic but spiritual—the blessings of the New Covenant. Jeremiah wrote materialistically; he communicated spiritually.

The Contemporary Prophetic Scene (23:9-40)

The Critique of the Prophets (23:9-15)

The prophet lamented the contemporary religious situation. It had deeply affected him mentally and emotionally: his heart was broken; his bones (personal stability) shook; he was like a drunken man. The occasion of this personal disturbance was the stern message of Yahweh that he bore and identified with as it came into contact with the deplorably antagonistic nation. He frankly pointed out that the land was full of adulterers whose infection contaminated the land and sterilized the pastures. Often the wickedness of humanity is dimensionalized in terms of agricultural or natural calamity (compare Lev. 18:25; Hos. 4:3). The nation's course was evil, and its power was misused. To illustrate, the prophet singled out two professions where righteousness might be expected; but no, both prophet and priest were ungodly even in the Temple ministry (vv. 10 ff.). The divine judgment was announced: their way would be like slippery paths in the darkness within which they would be driven and fall; evil would come upon them, for it was their hour of visitation (v. 12). Jeremiah then magnified the sin of the Judean religious personnel by comparing it with the now defunct Samaria. The prophets of Samaria were morally offensive in that they prophesied by Baal and led the people of Yahweh astray; but the greater horror was that of the prophets of Jerusalem: they committed adultery, lied, strengthened evildoers, and promoted moral defection. In a word, they were like Sodom and

Gomorrah (v. 13 ff.; compare Isa. 1:10) and were ripe for judgment, which was symbolically pictured as being fed with bitter wormwood and drinking poisoned water because from the prophets of Jerusalem ungodliness had gone forth into all the land (v. 15). It was a shocking reversal of their ordained mission!

The Critique of Contemporary Prophecy (23:16-22)

This poetic portion continues the tirade against the prophets, more particularly against their message. With the amazing injunction not to listen to the contemporary prophets, Yahweh condemned their message as one of vain hope, visions of their own mind, but not Yahweh's. They encouraged lawlessness by blessing the wicked and assuring them that no evil will befall them. These pretended prophets had never stood in the council of Yahweh, nor had they ever perceived or heard his counsel. The indictment continues: not only did they lack the authentic message of Yahweh, but they were never sent. They had never been called to be apostles, yet they ran self-appointedly. Yahweh had not given them his word, but they prophesied anyway. The truth is that if they had been in accord with the divine message, if they had stood in the council chamber of Yahweh, they would have proclaimed the divine message. That message was formulated to urge the nation to change its ways lest judgment follow. The false prophets proclaimed the opposite.

Further Critique of the Prophets (23:23-32)

In this oracle Yahweh indicated that he is both omnipresent and omniscient and, consequently, was perfectly aware of what was being perpetrated by the pseudoprophets. He had heard of their false professions to have dreams and in them the divine revelation. These dreams were merely self-projections of wishful thinking. They were indeed blatant falsehoods propagated by self-deceived clerics for their own ends. They had caused Yahweh's people to forget him even as the nation Israel forgot the revelation of Yahweh for the dreams and visions of Baal. Let the prophet, said Yahweh, who has a dream tell the dream, that is, state that it is a dream. But let him that has the divine word identify that world truthfully, for it is as wheat against the chaff of the false prophesying. The word of Yahweh is wheat, not chaff. The word of Yahweh is irresistible, like fire or as the hammer that breaks the rock in pieces. The divine word is able to cope with all that thwarts its way, to consume and pulverize the obstructions of evil, the false strongholds of entrenched evil, the pseudogospel of the false prophets. It is both liberating and judgmental, and in the latter role the self-deluded and mercenary prophets will experience its power.

The Burden of Yahweh (23:33-40)

Whether this portion came wholly from Jeremiah may be doubtful because of its long-windedness and repetition. The gist of this section centers in the double meaning of the term "burden." It denotes, on the one hand, "a thing borne, a load carried"; but, on the other, it has a technical meaning of a revelatory message (compare Nah. 1:1; Hab. 1:1). The prophet was instructed, when one asks him, "What is the burden of [Yahweh]?" to respond, "You are . . ."—exchanging the anticipated meaning of "burden" as "oracle" with its physical sense "burden to be borne." As such, Yahweh would cast them off. The term "burden" had suffered so much in usage that Yahweh enjoined that it shall no longer be applied to the divine message. Rather people who are inquiring of Yahweh, shall ask, "What has [Yahweh] answered or . . . spoken." Since "burden" had been misrepresented as signifying "burden" of Yahweh when, in reality, it was equal to every man's own word, those that confused the issue will be removed from Yahweh's presence, together with the city of Jerusalem, and both exiled to an unforgettable shame.

The Vision of the Two Baskets of Figs (24:1-10)

The setting of this oracle is after 597 BC, when the first captives were taken to Babylon. The exiled community consisted of the royal house, the nobles, and the upper artisan classes. The poor and unskilled were left in the land of Judah to prevent the land from deteriorating through fallowness and wild growth. As might be guessed, tensions developed between the two groups; and the question as to who would carry on the Judean fortunes became much more than an academic issue.

The Vision (24:1-3)

In the vision of the two baskets of figs placed before the Temple, Jeremiah, when asked what he saw answered that he saw two differing baskets of figs, one with very good figs, the other with uneatable figs.

The Interpretation of the Figs (24:4-10)

Yahweh explained the meaning of the good figs (vv. 4-7). They are the exiles in Babylon whom Yahweh will watch over and ultimately return to their homeland. He will build them up and not tear down, plant and not uproot them. Indeed, he will give them a heart to know that he is Yahweh. They will be his people, and he will be their God; for they shall return to him with their whole heart.

This is a most important pronouncement of Jeremiah concerning the role of the exiled community in Babylon. What residence in Judah could not accomplish, the Exile would. Moral regeneration, a two-way relationship with Yahweh, and a thoroughgoing repentance would characterize the exiles, the good figs, the hope of the nation.

The prophet now interpreted the meaning of the bad figs (vv. 8-10). They represent Zedekiah and his court, the remnant left in Judah, and those dispersed in Egypt. They will continue to degenerate until the final catastrophe falls and will become a horror, a byword, a taunt, and a curse wherever they go. Sword, famine, and pestilence would follow them until they perished.

This parabolic vision certainly did not enhance the popularity of Jeremiah with his fellow Judeans. No doubt, they considered it a bold slap in the face, a divisive and inflaming utterance, a most unpatriotic and treasonous word. The Judeans could have argued that since they were permitted to remain in the land of their fathers, were not they the favored of Yahweh? Was it not the filthy rich, the court, and the proud upper class that had caused all the trouble; and were they not now being punished in Babylon for their sins?

On the other hand, Jeremiah proved himself to be above favoritism and popularity. He would not pervert the divine message for personal reasons. Rightly had he interpreted the situation: the Exile would be redemptive for the deportees; they were the heart and hope of Israel. Such words were no doubt misinterpreted by the Judeans and ensured the animosity of the people toward Jeremiah.

Prelude to Universal Judgment (25:1-38)

Jeremiah Reviews His Ministry (25:1-7)

Jeremiah reflected upon his twenty-three years of service as a prophet to Judah (627-605 BC), a long ministry with precious little

to show for it save rejection. Despite his repeated and earnest efforts
to deter the people from their evil course, they had persisted in
their idolatry and wrongdoing.

The Resultant Judgment of Yahweh (25:8-14)

Yahweh had determined to use the services of Nebuchadnezzar to
punish his people (compare Hab. 1:5-11) and the surrounding
countries. The Babylonian invasion would devastate the land and
banish gladness, the establishment of new homes, industry, and the
production of the common necessities for a period of seventy years.
After this period, Yahweh would visit Babylon and punish her for
her iniquities. Jeremiah's oracles of doom would see their fulfillment
in Judah and the other lands against which he had prophesied.

Many scholars regard 25:1-14 as the end of the memoirs of
Jeremiah and compare the verses with 36:1-4, which is similar in
content. In the Greek translation (The Septuagint), dating from 200
BC, 25:13 is the introduction to the chapters dealing with the
foreign nations (chs. 46—51) while verse 14 is omitted altogether.
Once chapters 46—51 are complete, verse 15 continues the text.
This arrangement is more logical than the Hebrew text and should
be followed in studying the Book of Jeremiah. The interpretation of
verses 15-38 may accordingly be regarded as the conclusion of the
oracles against the foreign nations (chs. 46—51).

The Cup of Yahweh's Wrath (25:15-31)

Jeremiah heard the message to take from the hand of Yahweh the
cup of the wine of the divine wrath and to make the nations drink its
intoxicating contents (vv. 15 ff.). In compliance therewith, the
prophet administered the draft to the nations. Included in the list
are Jerusalem and Judah, its kings and court, Egypt with its nobility
and laity, and all the petty Palestinian states, the Phoenicians, the
Arabians, the kings of Zimri, Elam, Media, and the kings of the
north—in short, all the nations known on earth. Then, at last, the
king of Babylon shall drink also. The effect of the wine of wrath is
almost fatal in its inebriation. So, by implication, the drunken
nations will be plunged into a bloody war. They cannot escape either
participation in drinking the wine of wrath or the stupefying effect
thereof. Indeed, Yahweh would roar from on high against Judah and
the nations. The clamor would resound to the ends of the earth as he
entered into judgment with mankind and punished the wicked.

The Perilous Consummation (25:32-38)

Yahweh forecasted that evil was spreading from nation to nation leaving hosts of the slain in its wake. The rulers would be powerless to stay the spread of war or to attend to its sorry results. No refuge would be available either for royalty or laity. Amid general lamentation the land and homes would be devastated. Like a lion, Yahweh had left his thicket, and the lands would be wasted before his cruel sword wielded in fierce anger.

One can view verses 13-38 as a concluding summary to the oracles regarding the foreign nations and one that embodies a universal prospect involving the present or imminent control of the earth by the Babylonians and the fracture of the petty nations in that empire, and, ultimately, even the conqueror itself. Judah was part of that total complex. She must share in its fortunes, in its insane and drunken interrelationship, in its tragedy and suffering, yet never forget that wicked world was to be accepted and evangelized by the balm of Gilead resident in the promises of the God of Israel.

False Religion and Prophecy
26:1 to 29:32

The Sermon on the Temple and Its Sequel (26:1-24)

The Sermon (26:1-6)

This chapter begins the biographical accounts of Jeremiah provided by his secretary and biographer Baruch. The occasion parallels that of chapter 7, with this difference: in chapter 7 the contents of the sermon are much fuller than here; but the consequences of that sermon, omitted in chapter 7, are supplied here in detail.

The occasion of the address may be placed sometime in the early years of the reign of Jehoiakim (609-598 BC). Jeremiah was commanded to deliver in the Temple courts a stern warning to the congregating worshipers. Its purpose, as may be anticipated, was to urge his hearers to repent, to walk in the law, and to heed the words of his servants the prophets. If the admonition went unheeded, then the Temple would perish as did the tabernacle at Shiloh (1 Sam. 4:1 ff.; Ps. 78:60), and Jerusalem would become a curse for all peoples.

The Popular Reaction (26:7-9)

The words of Jeremiah caused a violent eruption from priests, prophets, and laity. They demanded the death penalty for blasphemy and indignantly repeated Jeremiah's words concerning the demise of the Temple and city.

The Judicial Trial (26:10-11)

Jeremiah was no doubt immediately arrested and sent to the royal court (compare Ps. 122:5), where the princes of Judah had convened. The charge preferred was no doubt treason against Yahweh and the state. The prosecution, represented by the priests and prophets, demanded the death penalty.

The Defense of Jeremiah (26:12-15)

Jeremiah's rebuttal was not a denial of his words, but an affirmation of his mission to Judah. He maintained that he had been sent by Yahweh to speak such words as he uttered against the Temple and against the city. His demands were correction of life and practice as the only certain alternative to disaster. The prophet abandoned himself to the judgment of the court, whether to be slain or to be freed; but he assured the audience that if he were put to death for his preaching, it would bring innocent blood upon the entire nation. Implicit in his defense was that, if they condemned him to death for his message, it would be more than just a homicidal miscarriage of justice; it would be the murder of an agent of God.

The Deliberation of the Sentence (26:16-19)

The princes who sat in judgment in the court were of a different mind than the religious prosecutors. They affirmed that Jeremiah was not worthy of death, for he had only performed his religious responsibility. Other defenders of the prophet, certain elders of the land, rose to his defense and cited the case of Micah of Moresheth. Micah had uttered a similar prediction concerning the city and the Temple and was not put to death by Hezekiah; rather a spirit of national repentance in Judah was created, and the threatened evil was thus averted (Mic. 3:12).

Legal Addendum: The Case of Uriah (26:20-24)

The biographer of Jeremiah related the triumph of his trial and that powerful pressures were exerted in the judgment by such influential men as Ahikam the son of Shaphan, who protected the prophet from the violence of the unthinking opposition. However, as a historian of the times, he did not wish to give the impression that all such trials ended in equitable verdicts. The seamy side of the reign of Jehoiakim was perhaps better exemplified by the case of Uriah the son of Shemaiah. This loyal prophet had uttered words closely akin to those of Jeremiah, but he paid with his life for his witness. Jehoiakim, the nobles, and the military sought to eliminate Uriah after they were told of his message. Fearful, Uriah fled into Egypt but was extradited by a royal embassy sent to Egypt for that purpose and was returned to face trial. The ruthless monarch slew him and desecrated his corpse by casting it into the burial place of the common people!

The Pantomime of the Yoke (27:1-22)

The same heading that introduced chapter 26 is found here. It places the present story somewhere about 609 BC, in the beginning of the reign of Zedekiah. The prophet was instructed to make thongs and yoke-bars and place them about his neck. The envoys of Edom, Moab, Ammon, Tyre, and Sidon had arrived in Jerusalem to formulate a united rebellion against the Babylonian rule. Jeremiah was to send word to deter them from the treasonable plot by directing them to tell their masters that Yahweh supported the present Babylonian lordship over the nations. Furthermore, he announced that any program to the contrary would meet with disaster. Accordingly, the religious personnel stirring up this rupture of relationship with Babylon were not to be followed. Stability could only be enjoyed by assuming the yoke of the king of Babylon (vv. 1-11).

Jeremiah addressed a personal admonition to Zedekiah to submit to the Babylonian king and to give no heed to the self-appointed and deceptive prophets, whose scheme would only destroy the nation (vv. 12-15).

The same advice was given to the priests and laity (29:16-22). They were not to be persuaded by the prophets who were predicting a speedy return of the vessels and, thus, the Exilic community now in the provinces of Babylon. To continue to serve Nebuchadnezzar was the only way to survive. He suggested that if the prophets had the word of Yahweh, they would pray that no further plunder of the Temple vessels occur. But this was wishful thinking, because Jeremiah's assessment of the situation was that the rest of the vessels now in the house of Yahweh would in due time be taken to Babylon as a result of the ruinous policies of state now in vogue. And yet, one day there will be a change. One day the vessels stolen from the Temple will be restored from Babylon.

One can see clearly in the thinking of the people the natural desire to see the overthrow of Babylonian power and the early return of the Temple furnishings, a yearning fanned into flame by the false hope the optimistic prophets were holding out to the discouraged people. It becomes clear what opposition Jeremiah's words would face as charges of treason, treachery, and unbelief would be hurled at him by the fanatic prophets.

The Opposition of Hananiah (28:1-17)

The Prophecy of Hananiah (28:1-4)

The stage was set in the fifth month of the fourth year of Zedekiah (594 BC) and was a reply to the yoke pantomime of Jeremiah (ch. 27). Hananiah the son of Azzur, the prophet from Gibeon, addressed the priests and the laity in the Temple with the glowing promise that Yahweh would return the furnishings of the house of Yahweh within two years as a result of the overthrow of the Babylonian power, and that Jeconiah (Jehoiachin), presently a hostage in Babylon, would be returned to Judah as would the exiles there with him. His thesis was that Yahweh had broken the yoke of the king of Babylon.

The Response of Jeremiah (28:5-11)

Jeremiah could not let this dangerous delusion go unchallenged. He might wish that such a course of events would take place, but, as he read the divine purposes, they were quite otherwise. After he spoke, he was willing to bide his time until the events themselves disclosed whether Hananiah or he spoke the truth. Hananiah's retort was to strip the yoke-bars from the neck of Jeremiah and to break them. He interpreted then the meaning of his action: So shall Yahweh break the yoke of Nebuchadnezzar within two years.

The End of the Matter (28:12-17)

After an interval of time the word of Yahweh came to Jeremiah commanding him to answer Hananiah more particularly. The prophet was to tell Hananiah that though he had broken wooden bars, bars of iron would replace them. Yahweh intended to support the regime of Nebuchadnezzar and any other proposed course conflicted with the purposes of Yahweh. Hananiah had disclosed himself to be self-appointed, without God's Word. He was in open rebellion against Yahweh in making the people believe a lie. Accordingly, the judgment had been decreed that Hananiah should be removed by death that very year. The postscript records the death of Hananiah two months later (v. 17).

Jeremiah's Letter to the Exiles (29:1-32)

Jeremiah dispatched a letter to the exiles in Babylon, including the priests, prophets, and laity, dated some time after the first deportation of Judah (ca. 597 BC). It was sent by the hand of Elasah the son of Shaphan and Gemariah the son of Hilkiah, envoys of Zedekiah to the Babylonian court. The letter admonished the exiles to build homes and families, to seek the welfare of the place where they were living and to pray for it, and not to believe the treasonous prophets and diviners, for they were fabricating false hopes. The letter continued with a hopeful note: when seventy years are completed, you will be returned home to fulfill the plans Yahweh has for your future. In that time the exiles will have their prayers heard; when they seek Yahweh, he will be found by them. Their restoration from the Dispersion will take place, and again they will dwell in their homeland. Here was national consolation for the future—but seventy years distant was a long time! (1-14).

Jeremiah then turned to protest against the regime of Zedekiah and the laity in Judah. They are vile figs and have consistently rejected the words of Yahweh sent to them through the prophets.

Their course was chartered for disaster, to be a curse, a terror, and a reproach among all the nations (vv. 16-19; compare 24:8-10). Jeremiah pronounced the divine word concerning the false prophets Ahab the son of Kolaiah and Zedekiah the son of Maaseiah who were creating havoc by their deceptive optimism advocating, no doubt, hope for the immediate fall of the Babylonian Empire and the immediate release of the exiles. These immoral men would be shown for what they were and would suffer appropriate punishment for their wickedness. It is then recorded that they were booked on charges of adultery by the Babylonian authorities and burned alive. They became proverbial for their infamy as examples of a just recompense for their evil deeds (vv. 21-23).

Jeremiah was enjoined to address Shemaiah of Nehelam. Shemaiah had sent a letter from Babylon to Zephaniah the son of Maaseiah the priest, to the priests and to the people urging them to restrain Jeremiah, insisting that Zephaniah had a duty to put every madman who prophesied madly in the stocks (vv. 24-28). He took violent exception to the length of the Exile which Jeremiah had indicated and to his advice to build houses and settle down in Babylon. The letter was read by Zephaniah to Jeremiah and received a stern repudition by the prophet. Jeremiah communicated to the exiles that Shemaiah was a very dangerous person and that his hopes were entirely unfounded. He was self-appointed and was opposing the divine plan by his deadly words. The judgment upon this false prophet and his house would be a premature death so as never to see the good which Yahweh had in mind for his people (vv. 29-32).

The Book of Consolation
30:1 to 31:40

The Promise of National Restoration (30:1-11)

At the divine command Jeremiah was to write in a book all the words that Yahweh had spoken to him. This concerns the words spoken regarding the restoration of the fortunes of the nation, both

Israel and Judah, when Yahweh would bring them home from their captivity in Babylon.

In poetic verse, the oracle begins with an auditory aside (a cry of panic was heard) as the question is asked whether a man can bear a child, for he is grimacing as a woman in travail. It was an incomparable day, a day of deep distress for Jacob, and yet he would be saved out of it (vv. 5-7).

A prose section follows in which Yahweh promised that the yoke of bondage would be broken from the neck of his people. No longer would they serve strangers, but they shall serve Yahweh and the restored Davidic monarch. In comforting words, Yahweh urged his servant Jacob not to fear, for he would save his people from their captors. They shall return to the Promised Land with none to frighten them because Yahweh will be there with his saving power. A full end may be expected of the nations among whom Israel is dispersed, but there shall not be a full end of Israel (compare 4:27; 5:10,18). Israel will, indeed, be disciplined, but that in just measure (compare 10:24).

"Wounded Now. Restored Anon" (30:12-17)

Yahweh examined his patient and frankly admitted that the nation's hurt was incurable and her wound grievous. None can help the situation; there was no cure-all available. All Israel's lovers (political allies) have forsaken her. The divine judgment had fallen in its severity upon his people. Well might Judah cry out in her misery, but it was but recompense for her guilt (vv. 12-15). This act of plundering by the Judean foes will not forever prevail; indeed, they who have pillaged Judah will themselves be spoiled. Yahweh would heal the wounds of the nation and give its foes the lie who dubbed Judah an outcast.

The Restoration of Zion (30:18-22)

In this oracle of the future consolation, Yahweh promised to restore the fortunes of Judah and rebuild the city and the royal house. Songs of thanksgiving and merriment will again be heard in

Zion. She will be multipled and honored as in the former days.
Yahweh will secure the continuance of his people and repel her
adversaries. David's descendant will emerge and minister (as a
priest) to Yahweh in privileged service. Judah will be the people of
Yahweh, and he will own them as his.

The Glory of the Latter Days (30:23 to 31:6)

The day of Yahweh with its stormy wrath will break upon the
wicked and fulfill the purposes of God. That purpose included the
restoration of the united Israel as the people of Yahweh. The
remnant that survives would experience the everlasting love, and
the nation will be rebuilt amid attendant joys and material prosperity. The day will come in the hill country of Ephraim when the
herald will summon its inhabitants to go to Zion to worship.

The Regathering of Israel (31:7-9)

An oracle similar to the foregoing celebrating more particularly
the restoration of Israel to her homeland introduces the subject. In
jubilant acclaim, both Jacob and the chief of the nations were to
glory in the fact that Yahweh had saved his people, the remnant of
Israel. He was about to bring them back from the north country and
from the distant parts of the earth. All of them, whether blind or
lame, mother with child or pregnant women (compare Isa. 40:11),
would return as a great company. With tears of joy they would
traverse the way. With provision for the journey and with easy
highways they shall return, for Yahweh is a father to Israel and
Ephraim, his firstborn.

The Heraldic Proclamation of Israel's Return (31:10-14)

Yahweh called the nations, even the distant coastlands, to hear this
word: He who scattered Israel, now gathers him. As a shepherd tends
his flock, so Yahweh has ransomed Jacob from the oppressors. Israel

would celebrate in song the goodness of Yahweh in the courts of Zion and the restoration of the natural bounty of the land. Life would be like a watered garden and care banished. Maiden and youth would rejoice in dance. The aged would join in the festivity, while the former mourning would be transformed into joy. Both priest and laity would be abundantly satisfied with Yahweh's goodness.

Elegy and Hope (31:15-22)

The depressing present moment cannot be denied. The hurt and wounds inflicted by the Babylonians and the heartbreak and humiliation of the Exile were present poignant experiences. The national sorrow was exemplified in the personification of Mother Rachel weeping in her ancient tomb at Ramah for her lost children. Now, in stark contrast, Yahweh commanded no further weeping, for Israel's work would be rewarded (Isa. 42:2). The people would return from the enemy's land to enjoy a new and bright future.

The sorrowful mood returns: Yahweh heard a lament; it was Ephraim bemoaning in penitential sorrow that Yahweh had chastened him like an untrained calf (v. 18). Now he ceased to kick against the pricks. Rather, he petitioned that he may be restored and own Yahweh's lordship.

Ephraim now turned to Yahweh (conversion) and repented (post-conversion repentance, that is, sorrow for a misspent life, compare Rom. 6:21*b*). When divinely instructed, he smote himself upon his thigh in shame because of his youthful disobedient ways. To respond to this penitential confession, Yahweh asked two questions: "Is Ephraim my dear son? Is he my darling child?" Both questions necessarily evoke a strong affirmative response. This same nostalgia continues as Yahweh confessed that as often as he had spoken against Ephraim, he always remembered him, and his heart yearned for him. Surely he would now have mercy upon him. It is a delightful monologue of Yahweh, a revealing self-disclosure, an exercise of love to bridge the alienation.

The mention of mercy prompts animated action. Yahweh commanded waymarks and guideposts be made for the journey along the highway which they would travel. Israel, though a faithless daughter, was not to waiver in a guilt-ridden dilemma, but to return to her cities, since Yahweh made the impossible dream possible.

The New Benediction (31:23-26)

Yahweh predicted that once more the land of Judah, presently suffering under the conqueror's heel, would again use its time-honored blessing: "[Yahweh] bless you, O habitation of righteousness,/O holy hill." When Zion's fortunes are restored, this good word will be eminently relevant and used as in former times. In that day Judah and all its cities will dwell contentedly. Weariness and weakness will no longer characterize their inhabitants. With this vision before him the prophet awakened as from a dream and adjusted himself to its happy dimensions (Ps. 126:1 ff.).

Restoration and the Individual (31:27-30)

Yahweh said that in the coming days Israel and Judah will increase in population and in their cattle holdings. No longer would Yahweh watch over them with evil intent, but he would watch over them to build and to plant (figures of a building and a garden). No longer would the nation suffer woes from the sins of the fathers; rather each would be individually responsible for his own personal sins. This last state foresees the day when the proverb, "The fathers have eaten sour grapes, and the children's teeth are set on edge" (compare Ezek. 18:2 ff.; Lam. 5:7) will no longer be current. The people will cease to blame their forebears for their own moral problem. Each individual will stand before God alone and will be responsible for his sin or his righteousness alone. Applied to the future restoration, it means that the previous generation will not indict the present generation. Rather people of each generation will be judged for their own ethical state.

The New Covenant (31:31-34)

With the same introductory formula as the preceding oracle, Yahweh promised that he would make a New Covenant with the house of Israel and the house of Judah. It will not coincide with the Sinai agreement, which Israel broke despite the close relationship between Yahweh and Israel. The new covenant may be divided in four prescriptions: (1) the inscribed law within the individual's mind;

(2) fellowship between Yahweh and his people; (3) an intuitive knowledge of Yahweh; and (4) the forgiveness of sin. The New Covenant will be inscribed in the heart of man, not written in cold stone. It will not be external to the individual. It will be internal. It will not be an authoritative command from without. It will be a personal motivation from within. It will not concern itself with the letter, but with the intent, the spirit, of the covenant. The knowledge of God will be empathetic; moral understanding will come from knowing God and, therefore, being like him. The knowledge will not be taught by instructors. It will be the product of the divine fellowship. In that covenant society the knowledge of Yahweh will be equally available, from the least to the greatest; and all will possess it. The building rests upon the cornerstone of divine forgiveness, a term not to be construed as solely negative, but embracing within itself all the saving benefits of divine atonement.

The question arises whether Jeremiah conceived this new relationship as something altogether future. There is no doubt that he believed the Exilic community during and after the Exile would participate in the New Covenant, but it would seem quite reasonable in view of all the data in Ezekiel, Isaiah 40—66, and the Book of Jeremiah itself to have been a reality present in the Exilic period and later. Every particular of the New Covenant has its parallel in Isaiah 40—66 and Ezekiel. Indeed, a recital of the redeemed life of the remnant in Exile is portrayed in the call, endowment, mission, and triumph of the Suffering Servant (Isa. 42:1-6; 44:1-5; 49:1,5-6; 52:13-13) and in the words of Ezekiel (36:25-27,31; 37:14). Indeed, the New Covenant is substantially repeated in 32:36-40 and 33:8. These promises were addressed to the Exilic community soon to be released from their Babylonian bondage and to return to the Promised Land. It would appear, then, that while the New Covenant was considered from one point of view as a future realization, it was decidedly a present reality in the experience of the dedicated.

There is within the structure of the covenant a limiting factor however: the covenant between Yahweh and the two houses of Israel. Jeremiah conceived the future restoration of Israel to have a universal significance in that God-fearing nations would become identified with the kingdom (or people) of Israel and as such would enjoy the spiritual blessings of Yahweh. The New Testament presents this important truth, that its benefits derive from Israel (Rom. 4:11-12,16-18; Gal. 3:14). It advances the thought, however, to identify the New Covenant as relevant to all mankind rather than to the "house of Israel and the house of Jacob" (Heb. 8:8-12; Gal. 3:8 ff.). The Old Testament prophecies in general were incomplete and imperfect. The full revelation came in the Son. The spiritual concept of the Suffering Servant, the elect nation of Israel, and other expressions of Zion's mission to the world have been fulfilled in the conception of the Christian church, wherein both Israelite and Gentile belong and unitedly may be designated the "Israel of God" (Gal. 6:16; Col. 3:11).

The Rebuilding of Jerusalem (31:35-40)

Yahweh promised that Jerusalem will be rebuilt and provided the details of the reconstruction. The valley of dead bodies, commencing with the brook Kidron to the corner of the Horse Gate toward the east, will be held sacred to Yahweh. It shall never be uprooted or overthrown. The memory of the disaster of 598 and 586 is here pictured as very sensitive to Yahweh and is enshrined as a consecrated memorial of deep significance suggesting permanence and inviolability of the Holy City.

The Restoration of Judah
32:1 to 33:26

Jeremiah's Purchase of a Field and Its Symbolic Meaning (32:1-44)

The Imprisonment of Jeremiah (32:1-5)

In 588 BC, when the Babylonians were storming Jerusalem, Jeremiah was apprehended by King Zedekiah for what the king imagined was treasonous preaching against the crown. He was taken as a prisoner to the court of the guard in the royal palace. Zedekiah, with his worldly-wise political views, considered Jeremiah a dangerous agitator; for the prophet had frankly stated that Jerusalem would be lost to Babylon, Zedekiah would be captured and confronted by the Babylonian overlord, and that further resistance would be futile.

Jeremiah's Redemption of his Patrimony (32:6-15)

The overture to purchase the land (32:6-8).—Hanamel the son of Shallum, the uncle of Jeremiah, visited the prophet in prison and asked him to purchase his field in Anathoth since Jeremiah had the prime claim to redeem it. Patrimony in Israel was zealously guarded within the family unit. When one wished to dispose of his land, he was bound by custom to offer it in accordance with the degrees of kinship. Jeremiah saw something more than the purchase of a field; to him it was the symbol of something much more significant. No one in his right mind would purchase property when the Babylonians were about to conquer the entire land. The land would have no value and would no doubt be parceled out as designated by the Babylonians (compare Mic. 2:4 ff.). And yet to Jeremiah the purchase of land, presently worthless, could become an eloquent pantomime to portray his faith that the land (and the people, too) had a future, that one day the seemingly foolish land purchase would be completely justified. This is what he confessed when he related the purchase to his message: "Then I knew that this was the word of [Yahweh]."

The culmination of the purchase (32:9-15)—The purchase of the property of Hanamel in Anathoth by Jeremiah was negotiated when the prophet was confined in the court of the guard in the palace of the king of Judah (32:2,12). Chapters 32 and 33 should be placed in that period. However, the confinement does not appear to have prohibited freedom of movement, since Jeremiah attempted to travel to Anathoth to finalize the conveyance of the property he had purchased. The text describing the latter incident indicates that Jeremiah was still going in and out among the people, for he had not yet been put in prison (37:4).

Jeremiah negotiated with Hanamel his cousin for the purchase of the redeemable property and agreed on a price of seventeen shekels of silver. The deed was signed, sealed, and witnessed, and the money was weighed in the scales. Jeremiah then took the sealed deed of the purchase (the clay tablet within the clay sheath) which contained the terms and conditions of sale, as well as the open copy (the tablet containing the inner document), and delivered the deed to Baruch the son of Neriah, the son of Maaseiah in the presence of Hanamel and the witnesses who signed the deed of purchase. All this was done in the presence of all the Jews who were sitting in the court of the guard. Jeremiah then charged Baruch before the audience: Yahweh commands you to take this sealed deed and this open deed (copy) and deposit them in an earthenware vessel that they may be preserved; for Yahweh says, "Houses and fields and vineyards shall again be bought in this land" (v. 15).

The Prayer of Jeremiah (32:16-25)

In his prayer Jeremiah extolled Yahweh as the great Creator of all, the loving God whose mercy embraces thousands, the omniscient God who sees the ways of men, the Lord of history who emancipated Israel from bondage and guided her to the Promised Land. But when Israel entered that land, she defected continuously from the ways of Yahweh, a disobedience that continued to the present. It would be punished by Yahweh. Now the thought changes to an associate idea: Why is it, asked the prophet, that you have commanded me to purchase a field which to all appearances is worthless, in a time when sword, famine, and pestilence abound in the city and siege mounds surround the walls, when a victory by the attacking Babylonians is inevitable?

The Response of Yahweh (32:26-44)

Yahweh admitted that Jerusalem would fall into the hands of the Chaldeans. The city would be burned, and the houses whose roofs were used to burn incense to Baal and to offer libations to other gods would be consumed. He acknowledged that Israel had been a problem since her youth, trafficking in idolatry and immorality until Yahweh's anger had been thoroughly aroused against all of Judah— the royal house, clergy, and laity. How could it be otherwise when they had done such evil to Yahweh. They had set up defiling abominations in his Temple and offered their children to Molech of Moab in unthinkable immorality. There had to be an end to all of this. The city would be plagued by sword, famine, and pestilence and given into the hands of the Babylonians. Yet this would not be the termination of the nation, for Yahweh would yet gather the dispersed and return them to their homeland. They would, however, become a different type of people. He would be their God, and they would be his people. He would bestow upon them a single heart and way so that they would reverence him for their own benefit as well as their children's. He would make with them an everlasting covenant never to turn away from doing good to them, but he would put his fear (true religion) in their hearts so that they, in turn, would not turn away from him. Yahweh would rejoice in doing good to them, planting them in their land in faithfulness with all his heart and soul.

This reply to the query of Jeremiah is the hope beyond the tragedy. In few passages is there such emotion on the part of Yahweh as he contemplated ministering goodness and love to a responsive people. He was altogether overjoyed despite the fact that the Babylonians would devastate Judah shortly.

The response turns then to the particular question of Jeremiah, Why do I feel divinely impelled to purchase a seemingly worthless field at such an unpromising hour? Yahweh replied that beyond the present evil there would be the promised good. In the desolation, devoid of man or beast, with the Chaldeans in utter control, it will happen that fields will be bought and deeds will be recorded throughout the Judean territory; for, says Yahweh, "I will restore their fortunes."

The Restoration of Jerusalem and Judah (33:1-26)

The chapter is a recital of the glorious restoration promised by Yahweh for his people. It is not unlike chapter 32 and essentially repeats some of the blissful future described earlier in the Book of Jeremiah. The setting of the oracle is the second encounter of Yahweh with Jeremiah while he was still shut up in the prison court (compare 32:1 ff.).

Yahweh declared in impressive, staccato sentences his creatorship and governance of the earth and urged the prophet call upon him and learn great and hidden things presently unknown. He then referred to the sorry condition of Jerusalem. The royal houses and the houses of the city had been torn down to provide a defense against the siege mounds the Chaldeans had erected. Notwithstanding their efforts, it was a losing cause because of Judah's immoral ways. The number of the dead would be enormous and the revelation of Yahweh mysterious (vv. 4-5).

But it will not always be so. After the disaster, Yahweh would restore the nation with prosperity and security as in the former years. The national sin will be cleansed, and Jerusalem will be a joyful name; indeed, it will be a praise and glory to all nations when they hear of Yahweh's goodness and provision (vv. 6-9).

The wasted places will be repopulated and the livestock abundantly replaced. Joy and gladness will be heard in the land. Family life will again be undertaken cheerfully; and the religious praises of the pious will be heard as they bring their thank offerings to the Temple, for Yahweh would restore the fortunes of Judah as at the beginning. Where there was now waste, without inhabitants, there will be dwellings of the shepherds pasturing their flocks through all the land of Judah (vv. 10-13).

Moreover in those days the promise to David (2 Sam. 7) will be fulfilled. A righteous Branch of the house of David will reign in righteousness, ensuring deliverance and security. Jerusalem will be called by its essential character: "[Yahweh] is our righteousness." Yea, David never shall lack a descendant to sit upon the throne of the house of Israel, nor shall the Levitical priests fail to have a representative to offer burnt offerings, cereal offerings, and to perform the sacrificial rites (vv. 14-22).

The question arises, Has Yahweh rejected his king and his people? (vv. 23-26). Yahweh called attention to a current punch line of the foreign peoples. They said he had rejected both Israel and Judah. Thus they do harm to his people and their future hopes. Yahweh responded by affirming that if his covenant with the day and night and with the astral ordinances can be broken, then he would also reject the descendants of Jacob and David his servant with none of his royal line to rule over the seed of Abraham, Isaac, and Jacob. The byword of the people is wrong. Yahweh would restore the fortunes of his people and have compassion on them.

Events in the Life of Jeremiah in the Reigns of Jehoiakim and Zedekiah
34:1 to 39:18

The Death of King Zedekiah (34:1-7)

This oracle's date may be roughly established about 587 BC, when Nebuchadnezzar was storming Jerusalem in particular and subduing

the Judean cities generally, with only Lachish and Azekah still
resisting (vv. 1,6 ff). Lachish is twenty-three miles southwest of
Jerusalem. Azekah is about eighteen miles west-southwest of
Jerusalem.

The oracle predicts that the Babylonians would capture and burn
the city of Jerusalem. Zedekiah would be captured, confronted by
the king of Babylon, and will be taken to Babylon. But he will die in
peace and be given an honorable funeral with the appropriate
rituals.

Duplicity in the Emancipation of the Slaves (34:8-22)

About 588 BC, when Nebuchadnezzar was besieging Jerusalem,
Zedekiah instituted an emancipation of all Hebrew slaves and
solemnized the edict with a covenant (vv. 10,15,18; compare Gen.
15:7 ff.). The royal house and the people enacted the decree and
released the Hebrew slaves, many of whom may have been retained
beyond the legal period of six years (Ex. 21:2; Deut. 15:12). The
release of all the slaves was considered that which was right in the
eyes of Yahweh. The extremes to which the Babylonians were
forcing the Judeans drove the king of Judah to do even more than the
law required. He hoped this act would move Yahweh to be merciful.

The siege was lifted momentarily by the Babylonians. The reason
may have been a threatening Egyptian invasion from the south or
some other similar reason. As soon as this happened, however, the
covenant was immediately annulled and the slaves that had been
freed were once again enslaved (vv. 8-11).

The response of Jeremiah was immediate and gave eloquent
expression to the righteous indignation that welled up within his
heart. Delivering an oracle in the name of Yahweh he denounced
this action in the strongest terms: treachery and perjury (vv. 15 ff.).
Yahweh, too, would proclaim liberty, said the prophet. He would set
loose his judgment: sword, pestilence, and famine; and the nation
shall be looked askance at by the kingdoms of the earth. Those that
transgressed the covenant would be like the covenant victims,
whether princes, priests, or people, and given into the hand of their
enemies to be devoured. Zedekiah and his house would be given
into the hand of the Babylonian king, for the determination of
Yahweh was to bring back the momentarily withdrawn Babylonian

forces to fight against Jerusalem and to burn it with fire, while the cities of Judah would be desolate without inhabitants (vv. 12-22).

Jeremiah and the Rechabites (35:1-19)

The Proffered Wine (35:1-11)

The Rechabites were generally associated with the traditions of Israel from the ninth century BC (2 Kings 10:15 ff.), when Jehonadab the son of Rechab associated himself with the revolution of Jehu. This ancestor of the Rechabites had prohibited the use of wine and the pursuit of an agricultural life for his descendants. This appears to have been a protest against the settled culture and an encouragement of a Bedouin nomadism in which their manner of life would be as undisturbed as their freedom.

When the army of Nebuchadnezzar and his allies (2 Kings 24:2-4) had fanned out through the entire land, the Rechabites sought refuge within the walls of Jerusalem. At his point, probably in the latter days of Jehoiakim (ca. 598 BC), the Rechabites were invited to one of the chambers in the Temple by the prophet Jeremiah. There Jeremiah set pitchers of wine before them and bid them drink. They replied that they would not disobey their forefather's command and refused to drink the wine.

The Object Lesson of the Rechabites (35:12-17)

The action of the Rechabites now became the thesis of Jeremiah's criticism of Judah. If the Rechabites through so many years have studiously obeyed their earthly father's command to abstain from wine, how much more should Israel obey the commandment of their God? But, alas, Judah had paid no attention to the divine commands. The servants of Yahweh, the prophets, had been sent with messages of repentance and change of life, but these have been studiously scorned. Accordingly, Yahweh was meting out the just recompense for such disobedience, the evil that he had pronounced against Jerusalem and the land of Judah.

The Reward for the Rechabites (35:18-19)

The Rechabites who had exhibited such exemplary conduct and true filial obedience to their ancestor's way of life were promised a perpetual posterity (vv. 18-19).

The Scrolls of Jeremiah (36:1-32)

The Command to Publish His Prophecies (36:1-8)

Jeremiah was instructed to write in a scroll all the oracles directed against Israel and Judah as well as those against the nations. The time covered would be from the days of Josiah in 627 BC, the year of the prophet's call, until the present, the fourth year of Jehoiakim (605-4 BC). It was a fitting occasion to publish the prophetic writings, for a day of national fasting had been chosen for their release. This fast was no doubt occasioned by the overrunning of Palestine by the Babylonians with the new monarch relentlessly pursuing his Egyptian foes and capturing cities such as Askelon which were loyal to Egypt. It was a moment of great danger and decision in Judah, for it, too, was an Egyptian tributary state. The solemn fast was accordingly instituted and may have had some bearing both on the repudiation of the Egyptian sovereign and the new pledge of allegiance to the Babylonians (2 Kings 24:1), as well as the acceptance of Judean fidelity by Nebuchadnezzar without military coercion (compare Zech. 7:4 ff.; 8:18 ff.).

The stated purpose of the reading of the prophecies was to warn Jeremiah's people again of the impending disaster if correction of life did not follow. Jeremiah complied with the divine command and dictated to his secretary Baruch the son of Neriah the oracles of Yahweh.

The Reading of the Scroll in the Temple (36:9-19)

Jeremiah was barred from the Temple for some unknown reason. He asked Baruch to read his words on the fast day when many Judeans would be present there. When Baruch had finished reading the oracles of Jeremiah, a certain Micaiah the son of Gemariah immediately reported their contents to the princes (state officials) of Judah who were present elsewhere in the Temple but had not heard the reading of the scroll. They sent Jehudi to bring Baruch and the scroll with him. When they heard the words of the scroll, they were alarmed and indicated that the matter was of such gravity that it must be reported to the king. They urged Baruch to hide himself, and to warn Jeremiah to do likewise, as they brought the scroll before Jehoiakim.

The Scroll's Rejection (36:20-32)

The princes reported all the words of Jeremiah to the king, who forthwith dispatched Jehudi for the scroll which had been deposited in the chamber of Elishama, the state secretary, for safekeeping. The king listened to the reading of the scroll; but when three or four columns were read, he cut them off from the scroll and threw them into the brazier before him until all the scroll was thus burned in the fire—despite the protests of some of his officers. Jehoiakim issued a warrant for the immediate arrest of Jeremiah and Baruch, but their hiding place was not discovered.

After this infamous event Jeremiah was commanded to rewrite the oracles of Yahweh, similar to those of the first scroll. To these he added many like words. For Jehoiakim's flagrant rejection of the words of Yahweh, Jeremiah predicted that the king would witness the victory of the king of Babylon over Judah and would have no successor to follow him on the throne of Judah but would experience with his people the woes that Jeremiah prophesied because of their evil ways.

The Imprisonment of Jeremiah and Visits by Zedekiah (37:1 to 38:28)

The Quest of Zedekiah for an Oracle (37:1-10)

The opening verses relate the elevation of Zedekiah to the throne of Judah and describe the national rejection of the message of Jeremiah. Zedekiah sent Jehucal the son of Shelemiah and Zephaniah the priest to Jeremiah to ask him to intercede with Yahweh in his behalf. At that time Jeremiah still enjoyed his freedom. The Egyptian pharaoh had marched out of Egypt, supposedly to aid the Judeans, and the Babylonians had withdrawn from Jerusalem. Jeremiah interpreted the new situation as no good for Jerusalem despite the momentary withdrawal. He warned that the Babylonians would return, capture, and burn the city. Zedekiah was counseled not to build up vain hopes because of the present Babylonian retreat, for they had the power and will to crush the Judeans.

Jeremiah Imprisoned as a Defector (37:11-15)

When the Egyptian army forced the Babylonians to withdraw, Jeremiah sought to visit his newly-acquired property in Anathoth but was arrested as a deserter to the Chaldeans at the Benjamin Gate. Despite Jeremiah's solemn protests, the arresting officer Irijah delivered him to the state officials who had him beaten and imprisoned in their rage (vv. 11-15).

The Second Mission of Zedekiah (37:16-21)

When Jeremiah had been a prisoner for many days in the house of Jonathan the secretary, which served as a prison, Zedekiah again attempted to contact Jeremiah and secure a divine oracle from Jeremiah. Asked whether there was a word of Yahweh available, Jeremiah replied that there was: Zedekiah would be delivered into the hands of the king of Babylon. The prophet took the opportunity to protest against his unwarranted imprisonment and asked the king why he did not consult his optimistic prophets who ruled out the Babylonian threat. Jeremiah added a humble petition that the king not send him back to his insufferable prison cell lest he die. The king granted him a much better prison and a daily ration of food.

There is something rather pathetic about Zedekiah: weak, vacillating, but not vile; seeking an oracle from Yahweh, but powerless to perform his duty; caught in the web of circumstances that would prove his undoing. Had times been otherwise, he might very well have been a friend of the prophet. At least, he gave him daily bread until all the bread of the city was gone, and that was stretching a point in favor of one whom the nobles had convicted and despised.

The Arrest of Jeremiah (38:1-13; compare 37:11-16)

Chapters 37 and 38 have considerable similarity and some differences, but it would seem that when all is considered that chapter 38 is an expansion of the details surrounding the arrest of Jeremiah and his subsequent imprisonment.

High governmental officials heard the proclamation of Jeremiah to the effect that desertion to the Babylonians was the one choice an individual had to save his life. Such disheartening words were regarded as treasonable. Jeremiah was seized, given a royal hearing, and sent to a prison compound. There, thrown in a muddy cistern, the prophet would have died shortly had not an Ethiopian eunuch, Ebed-melech, extracted him from the miry prison and then secured from the king a change of imprisonment.

The Mission of Zedekiah (38:14-28; compare 37:3-11)

Distrusting his powerful nobles, and bewildered at the worsening situation, Zedekiah sought a frank oracle from Jeremiah. The prophet hesitated at the request of the king. Were he to be candid, the monarch would put him to death; and if he were to give him advice, it would go unheeded. But Zedekiah again requested

Jeremiah to tell him all as to the present crisis and swore that
Jeremiah would not be harmed by communicating the truth. The
prophet then repeated his solemn warning that the only hope of
Judah was an immediate surrender to the Babylonians. Otherwise
total disaster faced the city with no possibility of escape. The king
did not appear to be surprised at the threatening oracle of Jeremiah;
but he was concerned that, if he did surrender, he might be given
over by the Babylonian king to the Judeans who had surrendered
and who might take vengeance on the monarch, whom no doubt
they blamed for the disaster. No, said Jeremiah, this will not
happen; your life will be preserved. If, on the contrary, you refuse,
the royal family will be taken captive and the city burned. The king
petitioned that his meeting with Jeremiah be kept in strict confidence and suggested a ruse to put off the prying inquiries of the
powerful officials of state. One can feel the instability of the throne of
Zedekiah and the suspicion and tension that existed in the last days
of the Judean kingdom between the king and his nobles and state
officials.

The Capture of Jerusalem (39:1-18)

In the ninth year of Zedekiah, in the tenth month, Nebuchadnezzar attacked Jerusalem. In the fourth month, on the ninth day, in
the eleventh year of Zedekiah a gap was made in the walls, and
Jerusalem fell. The city was then taken over by the chief military
officers of the Babylonians. The frightful and chaotic conditions that
prevailed may be imagined from the descriptions of Jerusalem's fall
and its aftermath in the Book of Lamentations. Frightened of the
impending events, Zedekiah and his elite guard attempted to escape
by night into the Arabah but were overtaken in the plains of Jericho.
He was taken to Riblah where Nebuchadnezzar was stationed.
There the Babylonian king slew the nobles, blinded Zedekiah after
he had slain his two sons before his eyes, and bound him over for
transport to Babylonian exile. Nebuzaradan, the captain of the
Babylonian guard, carried into exile the people who remained in the
city and those that had previously defected to the Babylonians.
However, he permitted some of the lower class to remain in the land
and gave them vineyards and fields to cultivate.

Jeremiah was released from captivity after the fall of Jerusalem.
Nebuchadnezzar had probably heard of the political views of

Jeremiah and issued orders that the prophet should be well treated. Accordingly, the high command released Jeremiah from his confinement in the court of the guard and entrusted him to the care of Gedaliah whom the Babylonians appointed as the new governor of the Babylonian province of Judah (vv. 11-14).

While Jeremiah was confined, an oracle came to him concerning Ebed-melech the Ethiopian, who had befriended the prophet and rescued him from certain death. The divine word was that despite the catastrophe of Jerusalem, Ebed-melech would be spared the captivity. He would be granted life because he had trusted in Yahweh. This trust may be identified as the kindness he had showed Jeremiah, even at the risk of severe reprisals from the pro-Egyptian party of officers (vv. 15-18).

Events in the Life of Jeremiah in Judah After the Fall of Jerusalem
40:1 to 43:7

The Release of Jeremiah (40:1-6)

After Jerusalem fell to the Babylonians in 586 BC, Nebuzaradan, the captain of the guard, released Jeremiah at Ramah from the captives destined to the Exile because of his pro-Babylonian political stance. The prophet was given the choice of journeying to Babylon or remaining in Palestine. Choosing the latter, he returned to Gedaliah, the newly-appointed governor of the province of Judah, and dwelt among the people who were left in the land.

The Ill-Starred Governorship of Gedaliah (40:7 to 41:18)
Gedaliah the Governor and His People (40:7-12)

When the surviving resistance forces of the Judeans heard that Gedaliah had been appointed as the Babylonian authority in Judah, Ishmael, Johanan, and other leaders of the beaten Judean forces met with him in Mizpah. The governor assured them that the Chaldeans would not take reprisals if they would only submit to the Babylonian

regime and that he would represent their interests before the new
authorities. He bid them dwell in the land and begin working their
farms again. The situtation was so favorable that some Jews who had
been scattered in the nations about Judah returned to harvest the
ripened crops. It seemed to be a promising new day after a
horrifying night of war.

The Threatened Assassination (40:13-16)

Whether this episode coincides with verses 7-12, or is a second
meeting with Gedaliah at Mizpah, remains an open question. At any
rate, the surviving military leaders, with Johanan acting as spokesman, admitted to the new governor that Ishmael, one of the Judean
princes, backed by the Ammonite king, Baalis, was plotting to
murder him and suggested that he stop the intrigue by nipping it in
the bud. However, the idealistic Gedaliah would not believe them
and dismissed the plot as a pure fabrication.

The Assassination of Gedaliah (41:1-9)

In the seventh month of his office (compare 39:2), Gedaliah
received a visit from the resentful Ishmael the son of Nethaniah, a
powerful member of the royal family and one of the chief officers of
the Judean king, together with ten associates. As they were eating in
Mizpah with the governor, Ishmael and his men murdered Gedaliah
and the Jews who were associated with the governor, as well as the
Chaldean soldiers who were stationed there.

On the following day eighty men from Shechem, Shiloh, and
Samaria arrived in mourning clothes at Mizpah on their journey to
Jerusalem, where with lament and sacrifice they intended to mourn
the pitiful fate of the nation before the ruined Temple of Yahweh. A
good actor, Ishmael went out to greet the pilgrims and invited them
to enter Mizpah and to greet the new governor. But once in the city,
Ishmael and his men fell on the pilgrims treacherously. They slew
seventy of them and tossed their bodies into a large cistern. The ten
who escaped the massacre did so by indicating that they knew the
whereabouts of precious stores of grain, a commodity sorely needed
by Ishmael.

The Attempted Flight to Ammon (41:10-15)

Ishmael gathered the rest of the Judeans in Mizpah, among whom
were Judean princesses, and set out for the safety promised in the

land of the confederate Ammonites. However, Johanan and the Judean military leaders heard of the deeds of Ishmael and engaged him in a battle at Gibeon. The Judeans Ishmael had forcibly brought with him fled to the forces of Johanan, leaving no alternative to Ishmael but to escape with eight of his followers to Ammon.

The Resultant Problem (41:16-18)

The question arose, now that Ishmael had fled, as to what to do in the perplexing political situation. Ishmael was certainly the culprit. He had murdered the Babylonian appointee Gedaliah and was now in the land of Ammon. Would the Babylonians seek reprisals against all the Judeans? Would not Johanan, a high ranking officer in the stout resistance forces of Judah, be blamed for the outrages at Mizpah? Would not Egypt with its peace, prosperity, and friendly relations with the Judeans be the logical place to find refuge rather than the devastated land of Judah now severely overcast with serious political troubles? Johanan and his forces led the people from Gibeon to the vicinity of Bethlehem, from whence they could make their way to Egypt.

The Political Turmoil after 587 BC

Why Ishmael slew Gedaliah can no longer be precisely determined, but a number of considerations may be suggested. From the devious behavior of Ishmael it is clear that he was an exceedingly treacherous and erratic leader, with all the savagery and cruelty of an irrational fanatic. He may have deeply resented the Babylonian appointment of Gedaliah, who was not of the royal family as was he, and the insufferable indignity of being subordinate in a new and hated regime. Gedaliah appears to have surrendered his forces to the Babylonians, but Ishmael was still in command of his troops in the open country. Did he consider Gedaliah a traitor to Judah, an opportunist, one who too quickly surrendered to the enemy and underestimated the vitality of the Judean resistance forces in the uncaptured cities and in the possible alliances with other Palestinian states beside Ammon?

But whatever may be said of Ishmael's political motivation and his fanatic patriotism—if that is what it was—his violence, his murder of the pilgrims, his treachery, and his exaggerated dedication to the resourceless Judean cause might well have produced the most

nightmarish future for the Judeans if he had not been forced to flee
for his life to Ammon.

The Inquiry of the Judean Fugitives and Their Flight to Egypt (42:1 to 43:7)

The Remnant's Inquiry (42:1-6)

Counsel in momentous decisions in Israel was sought from divine
oracles. Johanan, the military commanders, and the people petitioned Jeremiah to ascertain the mind of Yahweh and the directions
to follow. In a solemn exchange, Jeremiah promised to comply
wholly with their request, while they, on their part, swore that they
would fulfill whatever the oracle prescribed.

The Response of Jeremiah (42:7-22)

After ten days Jeremiah revealed the oracle of Yahweh in the
hearing of all of the assembled people. It directed that they should
remain in the land and that they might anticipate an optimistic
future. The Babylonian king was not to be feared. His attitude would
be one of sympathy with the past misfortunes of Judah. On the other
hand, if the people elected to go to Egypt, where they imagined
provisions and peace would be theirs, they would be sadly disappointed. The sword, famine, and pestilence would visit them there
until they had made an end of their posterity.

The oracle probably disappointed the military leaders and the
shallow optimism of the people. Jeremiah persisted in stressing
obedience to the divine word and insisted that as Yahweh's wrath
was lately poured out on Judah, so his anger would visit the Judean
should they enter Egypt. It would involve them in disaster, as their
contemporaries would plainly see. Yahweh had forbidden them to go
to Egypt, for it would only involve them in dire peril. The prophet
reminded the people that they had commissioned him to seek the
divine oracle; he had done exactly what they requested. If they
continued to disobey, disaster ultimately and surely would come
upon them.

The Opposition of the Leadership (43:1-7)

The reaction of the leaders to the oracle was immediate and
hostile. Azariah the son of Hoshaiah, Johanan the son of Kareah, and

their associates bluntly dubbed the words of Jeremiah a lie, questioned the integrity of his office, and attributed the negative character of the oracle to Baruch. It was an insolent response to the prophet's attempt to save the refugees from the inevitable confrontation with the Babylonians, which would mean death or exile if they were discovered as fugitives in exile. The commanders overrode Jeremiah and led the people into Egypt to the city of Tahpanhes and dragged the reluctant prophet with them.

Events in the Last Days of Jeremiah in Egypt
43:8 to 44:30

Jeremiah's Symbolic Action at Tahpanhes (43:8-13)

When the prophet Jeremiah arrived in Tahpanhes, he was instructed to enact a parable indicating the dire fortunes that would meet the Judean immigrants in Egypt. Taking large stones, he hid them in the mortar in the pavement around the entrance of Pharaoh's palace at Tahpanhes in public view of the Judean refugees. Then the prophet explained the reason for his action: Nebuchadnezzar, the servant of Yahweh, would one day set his throne and erect his royal canopy over these stones. Indeed, the prophet affirmed, the Babylonian king would destroy the Egyptian temples and take its people captive. Accordingly, the Judeans would not be immune to the danger of the Babylonian power, despite their trek to their new residence in Egypt.

Nebuchadnezzar invaded Egypt in the thirty-seventh year of his reign (568-7 BC) and defeated Pharaoh Amasis. The details of the encounter are very sketchy. Two conclusions may, however, be drawn. The Babylonian monarch did not wish to establish a permanent sovereignty over Egypt, but apparently sought to thwart Egypt from interfering in Asian affairs, and the Egyptians maintained peaceful relations with Babylon after the military operation of 568 BC. On the whole, these events would tend to establish Jeremiah's reputation as a prophet. They partially fulfilled his prophecy concerning the Babylonian supremacy over Egypt in the days after the Judean refugees arrived in Egypt (compare 46:13-26).

Jeremiah's Rebuke of the Refugees' Worship of the Queen of Heaven (44:1-30)

The Rebuke of Paganism (44:1-6)

Jeremiah delivered what may have been his final address to his Judean contemporaries in Egypt, as they gathered from the cities where they had settled. The prophet pointed out the ill-starred experience of their fathers in idolatry and in the service of other gods, despite the continual warning of Yahweh's servants the prophets and their passionate pleas to cease such practices, and how the divine wrath fell upon the Judeans through the Babylonian invasions and captivities.

Exhortation to Renounce Heathenism (44:7-10)

If the Judeans now in Egypt commit the same sins as their fathers, they will also share a similar fate. In three ponderous questions the prophet pointed out the folly of their persistent defection and inquired whether they wish to be consumed in their wickedness by continuing the abominable practices of their forebears.

The Judgment Announced (44:11-14)

The prophet predicted that the remnant in Egypt would be consumed by war, by famine, and become notorious in the eyes of the contemporary world. They would be dealt with in the same judgmental ways that their fathers experienced, with no survivors left among them.

The Idolatrous Judeans' Reply (44:15-19)

The words of Jeremiah were contested by his audience. The women who were devotees of the Queen of Heaven and burned incense to her shrine and performed other ritualistic devotions in her service took violent exception to the words of Jeremiah. They stoutly maintained that the prophet had completely misunderstood what had happened in Judah. They insisted that when they had worshiped the astral deity, before the radical reformation of Josiah, all was prosperous and well; but once he stopped their religious services, all the present calamities fell upon the nation. All this was a sure sign that the Queen of Heaven had been offended by the ending of their adoration and had inflicted her wrath upon the Judeans through the Babylonian disaster. Two interpretations, diametrically opposed, were thus stoutly presented; and to the followers of each, their own view was so compelling, so simple, so right. The heated argument did not end there, however. The women vowed that they would renew their former worship of the Queen of Heaven, burn incense, and pour out libations to her, as they had done in the good, old days, despite Jeremiah's denunciations.

The Response of Jeremiah to the Idolaters (44:20-30)

Jeremiah retorted that the judgment of Yahweh was the cause of the present disaster, which in turn was due to the idolatrous practices and abominable evils of the Judeans, not the least his present opponents. Furthermore, he added, the insolent women who proposed to continue their adoration of the Queen of Heaven would bring the further judgment of Yahweh upon the Judean remnant, and then the moment of truth would arrive; they would know who was speaking the truth and who was telling the lie. An oath of Yahweh had been sworn against the Judeans now in Egypt that they would be exposed to the sword and famine, while those that escaped to Judah would be pitifully few. The divine sign of this would be the ouster of Pharaoh Hophra, who would be given into the hands of his enemies; in this case it proved to be Ahmosis II (Amasis) who assassinated him in 569 BC. The instability of Egypt in the wake of this overthrow of the pharaoh would be the sign and cause of the Judeans' woe and judgment.

The Admonition to Baruch
45:1-5

In the fourth year of Jehoiakim (605 BC), when Baruch, the secretary of Jeremiah, had written at the dictation of Jeremiah the words of his prophesyings (compare ch. 36), an oracle of Yahweh came to the prophet concerning Baruch. It appears that the secretary of Jeremiah was deeply troubled; whether by the dangers of his task or the seeming fruitlessness of his work, self-pity, or a mercenary concern, is not disclosed. The oracle asked Baruch to see the nature of the times: that Yahweh was breaking down old structures and plucking up discardable elements throughout the land. It was a period of turmoil and confusion, of instability and consternation, of old matters being replaced by new things. It was not a time for self-seeking, for personal advantage, for self-interest, not when the world was in flames. It should be quite enough that Baruch was permitted to live, and that assurance was granted to him as a prize of war wherever he was to go. It was better to be a live dog rather than a dead lion; and Baruch should be sensitive to the favor of life and pay less mind to honors, gains, and self-exaltation.

The chapter is a frank acknowledgment that even among the great religious personalities the cross of Yahweh is not always borne triumphantly and joyfully. At times, we do not seem to be getting anywhere; the struggle takes our energy, and little relief or hope appears on the horizon. Both Jeremiah and Baruch had such moments of self-pity and despondency. Yet the experience of the prophets, when the tale was told, was this: the resilience of the converted soul.

> Rejoice not over me, O my enemy [person or thing]; when I fall, I
>   shall rise;
> When I sit in darkness [Yahweh], will be a light to me (Mic. 7:8).

Oracles Against the Foreign Nations
46:1 to 51:64

The oracles against the foreign nations in the Book of Jeremiah occupy chapters 46 through 51 in the Hebrew text. On the other hand, in the Septuagint, these oracles are inserted between Jeremiah 25:13 and 25:15 with verse 14 being omitted. Moreover, there is a direct relationship between Jeremiah 25:15 and following and the oracles against the foreign nations. These oracles appear to have been a separate entity which was introduced later into the Book of Jeremiah. They were generally written with reference to the period 605-561 BC and address themselves to six nations. They may be compared with similar oracles in Isaiah 13—23, Ezekiel 25—32, Amos 1—2, and the fourth oracle of Balaam (Num. 24:15-24).

The significance of the oracles directed against the foreign nations may be seen in that they expressed the considered attitude of the prophetic party in Israel/Judah. One cannot underestimate the influence of the prophetic movement in the history of Israel. The prophetic element entered into the life of the nation very early. Samuel was acclaimed as the prophet of Yahweh and brought to his office the integrity, independence, and success of a great political and religious figure. From that vantage point he could initiate a royal form of government and nominate the first king. When that king disappointed him, he had the power to replace him with another dynasty. From that time onward the power of the prophetic party was established as a primary force in religion, politics, social, and religious concerns. Even at their weakest times, they still were powerful voices and leaders within the nation and represented a segment of national opinion that could not be ignored.

Another feature that must be introduced here is the international relations which must have existed from the very start of the national life under the monarchy. There must have been foreign embassies in Jerusalem, staffed with a diplomatic corps to articulate political, social, and economic affairs of state. That envoys arrived in Jerusalem from foreign countries (27:3) and that envoys were dispatched by the Judean king to foreign capitals (2:36 f.; Ezek. 17:15) does not deny the existence of resident foreign embassies in Jerusalem. It would follow that Israel/Judah would likewise have their foreign diplomatic corps located in embassies in foreign countries. Such international, diplomatic establishments provided not merely for political and economics ends. They were effective listening posts, gathering data for their own countries and communicating the news to the home government. Accordingly, when such an outstanding statesman as Jeremiah the prophet spoke, he was a voice to be heard. He represented a powerful minority in Judah and, like all other prophets, he gave considerable attention to political analysis, both domestic and foreign, and would be a significant leader in the formulation of political policy and international relations.

It may be assumed, then, that these oracles are by a keen political analyst, backed by a powerful prophetic minority, and influential beyond their numbers. They are a critique of the six foreign nations and must have been carefully studied by each of the respective governments. The oracles were not empty, meaningless utterances. They were prized documents of state concern.

However, one should not imagine that the oracles will read like modern documents. They have to be compared with political documents, from the ancient Near East of that particular time.

Against Egypt (46:1-28)

The Invasion of Egypt, Part 1 (46:1-12)

In May or June 605 BC, the newly-crowned king of Babylon, Nebuchadnezzar, defeated Neco II of Egypt at Carchemish on the northern Euphrates, some six miles west of Haran. He pursued the Egyptian army to the borders of Egypt.

After a general introduction to the oracles against the nations (v. 1), the focus turns to Egypt and the defeat by Nebuchadnezzar that had been inflicted in 605 BC. In the satirical and martial oracle, Egypt was encouraged to prepare her forces for the encounter with full battle equipment. But, alas, it was all spent in vain! The Egyptians panicked and hastily retreated; the army was shamefully defeated. Egypt with its proud, boasting hosts advanced with arrogant confidence, but Yahweh determined the outcome: the sword of their enemy devoured them. No medicines, no therapeutic measures will heal the wounds Egypt had received. The nations have heard of the shameful defeat.

The Oracle Against Egypt, Part II (46:13-26)

The superscription identifies the sequel as an oracle of Yahweh concerning the invasion of Egypt by Nebuchadnezzar. The composition begins with a prescription to publish in the Egyptian Delta (Migdol, Memphis, and Tahpanhes) the military alert against the Babylonian power. But, again, Egypt is routed. Their animal gods provided no assistance. Their multitude stumbled and fell as they retreated hastily before the invader. Yahweh had decreed the defeat. Sarcastically, the name of the pharaoh is dubbed the "Noisy One Who Lets the Hour Go By," which, put into our modern idiom, would be "The Loud Mouth Who Missed the Boat" (vv. 13-17).

The second stanza of this poem continues with an affirmation that one as monumental and unique as the mountains of Tabor or Carmel shall come against Egypt. Such an announcement from Yahweh urged Egypt to prepare for this catastropic invasion, devastation, and exile. Egypt is likened to a beautiful heifer which is severely tormented by a gadfly from the north (Babylon). Her mercenary soldiers, whom she parades with such pride, have turned and fled in the day of calamity. The retreat of the Egyptian forces resembled a serpent gliding swiftly away. Her enemies march in force, and, like those who fell trees in a forest, they will stop at no obstacle but will level Egypt to the ground despite her boasted strength. The invaders were more numerous than locusts. Indeed, before such titanic power Egypt would be deeply humiliated and delivered into the hands of a people from the north (the Babylonians, vv. 18-24).

The third part of this section (v. 25 f.) is unlike the previous two (vv. 2-12; 13-24). It is prose and has reference to Thebes in Upper Egypt. It predicts that Yahweh's judgment will come upon the religious pretense of the Egyptian gods and on her kings and those that trust in them. They shall all be delivered into the hand of Nebuchadnezzar and his hosts. Yet, despite the disaster, Egypt would recover and be restored as in the days of old.

An Oracle of Comfort (46:27-28)

This word of Yahweh is in the spirit of Isaiah 40—66 and is designed to comfort the exiles by holding out the promise of restoration and prosperity. It is quite similar to Jeremiah 30:10-11 and, apart from verse 26b, is employed here to contrast the destruction of Egypt with the reconstruction of all Israel.

Against the Philistines (47:1-7)

The superscription of the oracle indicates a date somewhat before Pharaoh smote Gaza. The Septuagint retains only the words: "Concerning the Philistines." While the encounter mentioned in the superscription may be safely located some time in the early years of the seventh century BC, there is no historical data by which to be more precise.

The foe from the north will overflow the land as an overflowing torrent (compare Isa. 8:7 f.). The reaction of the threatened population is vividly described in verse 2 and following. Men shall cry out. The inhabitants shall wail. The fathers will be unconcerned with their children, so distraught are they at the approach of the military might of the enemy with its prancing horse cavalry and its deadly, raging chariots. The enemy will invade the western land. The Philistines, the Phoenicians, and her allies, indeed, all shall be devastated by the invasion—an action supported by the order of Yahweh and the sword of his judgment.

Against Moab (48:1-47)

The occasion of this oracle cannot be determined with any precision. The invaders are either the Assyrians or, more likely, the Babylonians. In 601 BC the Babylonians staged punitive raids against Moab (2 Kings 24:1-4; compare 27:2-11); in 594 Moab was involved in a treasonous plot against Babylonian rule.

The first oracle begins with a woe directed against four areas of Moab. Two are now laid waste; the other two momentarily await a similar fate (vv. 1-2).

The second stanza describes the lament occasioned by the destruction (vv. 3-5) and the immediate orders to flee from the foe, as from certain destruction. The strongholds, the national wealth, the god Chemosh, and its clergy will provide no support against the threatening disaster of doom and exile. Nothing will exempt the urban centers and rural areas. Both shall be destroyed in accordance with Yahweh's word. His ministers of judgment will not slacken their efforts in their appointed duties (vv. 8-10).

The third stanza pictures Moab as a country with an undisturbed history, without political tragedy or exile. Appropriately for a rich, wine-producing land (v. 32 ff.; Isa. 16:8-11), the author compares Moab to wine that remains permanently in one position, unpoured from vessel to vessel, but resting on and absorbing the bitterness of its dregs. Yahweh is about to commission tilters who will tilt the position of the casks; indeed, they will break the wine jars in pieces. This shattering of the nation will deeply embarrass the national honor of the god Chemosh and prove to be as humiliating as the impotence of Bethel was to Samaria. Such mortification as will befall Moab prompts the poet to pose a poignant question: "How do you say, 'We are heroes and mighty men of war'?" Why, the destroyer of Moab is on his way, and the flower of the nation shall perish, so says the King, the Lord of hosts. With calamity so near, the sole fitting mood is lamentation that the former glory is now lost. Dibon, the capital, is bidden in such straits to descend "from her glory," her royal throne, (compare Isa. 47:1 ff.), and, like a captive, to sit on the parched earth in view of the devastation of the invader. The inhabitant of Aroer, another city of Moab, now comes into focus as she inquires of the fugitives as to what has happened. Moab is so battered and humiliated that the auditor is bidden to wail and cry, to tell by the brook Arnon the horrendous happenings: Moab is wasted!

In the fourth verse, which is written in prose, the destruction of the various cities of Moab is mentioned, indicating that the power of the Moabite kingdom is over (vv. 21-25). In the fifth stanza, also in prose, the motif of intoxication is introduced. Make Moab drunk that he may magnify himself against Yahweh to his own defeat and derision. The author suggested that the derision will be permanently the humiliation of Moab and will be a fair exchange for the reproach with which she had derided Israel.

The sixth stanza urged Moab to imitate the mourning doves. The insolence of Moab, her deceptive boasts, and her treacherous practices draw a pathetic response even from Yahweh. Pictured again as a center of grape growing, Moab, the vine of Sibmah so extensive in its growth, will be destroyed (compare Isa. 16:8-14). Gladness will be removed from the fruitful land of Moab, and the wine presses will be closed and their personnel silent (vv. 28-33).

The seventh stanza portrays the saddened scene amid the cries of anguish throughout Moab for the failing of the waters of Nimrim, all of which refers to the outcry of the inhabitants of Moab because of the devastation of their country. To this physical woe is added a spiritual one: Yahweh promises that the religious ceremonies in Moab will also cease. These words draw a passionate lament from the poet similar to the mournful notes of the flute, since the wealth of Kir-heres (Moab) has perished (vv. 34-36). The signs of mourning were everywhere—people with heads shaved, beards cut, hands gashed, and loins girded with sackcloth. Yahweh had broken Moab like a vessel, forsaken and fragmentized. With wailing and in shame Moab had become a derision to her neighbors (vv. 37-39).

This eighth stanza foresees the invader coming with the speed of an eagle against Moab. The nation would no longer be a people because they had magnified themselves against Yahweh. There was nothing in view for them except terror, pit, and the snare which will soon engage them in their toils (vv. 40-43). Escape will be impossi-

ble in the time of Yahweh's visitation (v. 44; compare Amos 5:19).
Fugitives are pictured stopping in the way without strength to go on,
as the nation of Moab is desolated. Woe is Moab, the people of
Chemosh, for her inhabitants are taken captive (vv. 45 ff.).

The final verse of this poem against Moab predicts the ultimate
restoration of the fortunes of Moab. In the final verse of this tirade
against Moab, Yahweh promised that in the latter days the present
misfortunes will be reversed (v. 47).

Against the Ammonites (49:1-6)

The oracle forecasts the doom of Ammon, her capital, her towns,
and her god Milcom because the Ammonites dispossessed the tribe
of Gad to take its cities for themselves. This seems to have been
standard procedure for the kingdom of Ammon, since Amos com-
plained about their cruel property taking in his days, (Amos 1:13;
compare vv. 3-5, where the same malpractice is attributed to Syria).
An unnamed invader will desolate Rabbah, the capital of the
Ammonites, and burn its villages with fire; then the Gadites will
repossess their land (vv. 1-2).

In view of the impending disaster, Heshbon, Ai, and Rabbah
(chief cities of Ammon and symbolic of the total nation) are urged to
lament and put on mourning garb. It is particularly calamitous since
Milcom (literally, king), their god, with his priests, together with the
royal house will share in the captivity and exile (compare Isa. 46:1 f.).
All this forms such a contrast to the imagined security: their
agricultural wealth, their treasures, and their pride which asked
arrogantly, "Who will come against me?" (v. 4). Yahweh would bring
terror upon Ammon (vv. 3-5). The oracle ends with the same hopeful
promises granted to Moab (compare 48:47) and to Elam (49:39).

Against the Edomites (49:7-22)

The announcement of disaster which will befall Edom begins with
a sarcastic inquiry whether "wisdom" (here to be interpreted as
"shrewdness"), so proverbially associated with Teman, has utterly
vanished (compare Obad. 8) so that the impending doom is
unrecognized. The poem then urged the inhabitants of Dedan (a
city in Moab) to flee from the coming disaster, one that will be far

more devastating than a plundering attack for booty and from which there will be no escape (vv. 8-10). Edom is advised to leave the orphan child and widow that survive the disaster to the care of Yahweh, for no one else will be there to care for them.

Again the oracular introduction: "thus says [Yahweh]," proceeds with a question: If those who did not deserve to drink the cup (of Yahweh's wrath; see 25:15; Isa. 51:17,22) must necessarily drink it, how much more shall they drink of the cup who deserve to do so? Bozrah, a great fortress city in Edom, will become a horror and accursed; indeed, all her cities shall be perpetual wastes (vv. 12 ff.).

Tidings of Woe (49:14-16)

This poetic portion represents the prophet hearing tidings from Yahweh concerning the attack which the nations will make upon Edom. The result will be to destroy and defame the nation. All her imagined security in her mountain fortresses will not save Edom from this woe (compare Amos 9:2-4; Obad. 2 ff.).

The Future of Edom (49:17-22)

The future of Edom is pictured in this prose section (vv. 17-22) as resembling the notorious fate of Sodom and Gomorrah, bereft of inhabitants and overthrown. The assault will be as sudden as the attack of a lion on a sheepfold; no shepherd (king/ruler) will withstand the onslaught; and Yahweh will cause the sheep (the inhabitants of Edom) to be scattered and to be gathered by new shepherds appointed by Yahweh. The purpose that Yahweh has for Edom will involve the land in appalling disaster. Her cry will be heard as far as the Red Sea (v. 21). Even now an unnamed foe will fly swiftly against Bozrah, and the warriors of Edom will be demoralized (vv. 22).

The close relationship between Jeremiah 49:7-16 and Obadiah 1-8 raises the question of literary dependence. Did Obadiah produce the verses and Jeremiah adapt them (most likely); or was it vice versa? Of course, both could have borrowed from an early writer.

Concerning Damascus (49:23-27)

Aram, later known as Syria, was located to the north of Israel; its capital was the great city of Damascus, and the region boasted of other great centers such as Hamath and Arpad. The name of its monarch was generally Ben-hádad, that is, the son of the god Hadad. The cities of Hamath and Arpad are represented in this oracle as hearing evil tidings and melting in fear, as a woman in travail with anguish and sorrow. The famous city of Damascus is seen as forsaken; her youth are fallen in her squares; her soldiers will be destroyed in that day, says Yahweh, when he kindles a fire in the wall of Damascus which will devour the palaces of Ben-hádad.

Concerning Kedar and the Chieftains of Hazor (49:28-33)

Kedar represents a powerful Arabian tribe (Isa. 11:16 f.; 42:11; 60:7; Jer. 2:10) and the chieftains of Hazor the unwalled cities where the Arab tribes settled. It cannot refer to the city north of Israel; but in its mention with Kedar it would appear to be in Arabia. Kedar was famous for its sheep breeding (Isa. 60:7), its trade with Phoenicia (Ezek. 17:11), and for its famous archers (Isa. 21:16 ff.). Both Kedar and Hazor were smitten by Nebuchadnezzar in 599 BC.; this oracle appears to be anticipation of that disaster. It bids an unnamed foe (the Babylonians) to advance against Kedar and to destroy it, taking its tents, flocks, curtains, and camels as booty. The inhabitants will cry aloud as the raiders close in, "Terror on every side!" (6:25; 20:2 f.,10; 46:5). Yahweh counseled the inhabitants of Hazor to flee before Nebuchadnezzar and his contemplated attack. He pointed out the defenseless status of Kedar and Hazor—Bedouin folk dwelling in ease, with no city gates or bars. Their camels will become booty, their herds a spoil, their inhabitants fugitives.

Concerning Elam (49:34-39)

Elam is situated east of Babylon, and the oracle is dated in the superscription in 597 BC, in the beginning of the reign of Zedekiah. Yahweh forecasted breaking the bow of Elam, the mainstay of their military might, and scattering Elam to the four winds among all nations. Elam will be terrified before her enemies. Evil will come upon her until the sword liquidates the nation. Yahweh would set his throne in Elam (that is, totally in control) and would destroy the ruling class. But, as in two previous oracles (49:6; 48:37), Yahweh will restore the fortunes of Elam in the latter days (v. 39).

Concerning Babylon (50:1 to 51:64)

This major oracle concerns the most important contemporary nation, Babylon, to which the Judeans were subjected from 605 BC until the rise of the Persian power in 538 BC. In splendor, culture, sophistication, wealth, military might, architecture, fine arts, learning, astronomy, law, and literature, the Babylonians continued the superb tradition of the Sumerian-Akkadian culture and attained an eminence beyond their predecessors.

Babylon's Fall and Israel's Release (50:1-10)

This oracle begins with a command to publish the ominous news that Babylon is taken, its gods Bel and Merodach (Marduk) have been defamed, and their idols humiliated. This catastrophe had been caused by an unnamed foe which had come against her and devastated her land (vv. 1-3). In this moment of Babylonian reverses, Israel and Judah shall come unitedly with penitence to seek Yahweh their God. Inquiring the way to Zion, they will join themselves to Yahweh in an everlasting covenant (v. 4). Yahweh declared that his people have been like lost sheep; their shepherds (rulers) have led them astray to become the prey of their enemies who excuse their own predatory ways by using the sin of Israel as their justification (vv. 5-7). Israel now is bidden to flee from Babylon, for Yahweh is stirring up such opposition against Babylon that it will surely be plundered (vv. 8-10).

The Demise of Babylon and the Restoration of Israel (50:11-20)

Babylon, the plunderers of his heritage, was warned by Yahweh that despite present wantonness in their imagined security, the people that began the nation will be disgraced and the nation utterly shamed as "a wilderness dry and desert" (v. 12). From another vantage point, the poet uttered an encouragement to the foe attacking Babylon to have their archers set themselves in array and shoot at her, for she had sinned against Yahweh; to raise a cry against her for her bulwarks have fallen. Yahweh had taken vengeance on Babylon, and her vast agricultural wealth would cease; then when the oppressor obtained all, he shall flee back to his own land (v. 16).

The oracle continues with Israel being described as sheep driven by lions, Assyria first, then Nebuchadnezzar; but neither would go unpunished. Yahweh will restore Israel to her land and forgive her sin (vv. 17-20).

Babylon, the Hammer of the Whole World (50:21-32)

In this oracle against Babylon the invader was bidden to go against the land of Merathaim (the confluence of the Tigris and the Euphrates) and against the people of Pekod (eastern Babylon), there to slay and destroy. The resultant action would bring the noise of battle and great destruction on the "hammer of the whole earth" (Babylon). The mighty nation had become a horror; she had been taken unaware because she had striven with Yahweh. He has opened his munitions, the weapons of his wrath against the land of the Chaldeans. The foe was invited to open the Babylonian granaries, utterly to destroy the nation, and bring the cattle (perhaps idols; Isa. 46:1) to the slaughter, for it was a day of woe.

There is a momentary break in the martial tone of the poem, and the announcement is introduced that the Israelitic exiles are fleeing from Babylon (Isa. 48:20; Jer. 51:6) to declare in Zion the vengeance of Yahweh for the destruction of his Temple (v. 28).

Again the martial tone resumes, this time in prose. It summons archers to surround Babylon and to take vengeance for all her misdeeds and for her defiance of Yahweh. The result will be the slaughter of her youth in the squares and the destruction of all her soldiers (v. 29 ff.). In verses 31-32 the announcement is made that Yahweh was pitted against Babylon, that her day for judgment had come, with the proud stumbling and the cities burned.

An Oracle of Hope for Israel (50:33-34)

A promise is made here to Israel and Judah that the present bonds that hold them in captivity to Babylon would soon be broken. The Redeemer of Israel, the strong Yahweh of hosts, would surely plead Israel's cause when he gives rest to the earth and unrest to the disquieting Babylon.

An Oracle of the Sword (50:35-40)

Five times the word *sword* introduces a new line in this oracle. While the precise identification of the sword is not given, it appears that it is the sword of Yahweh exercised in judgment against Babylon. It is pitted against the Chaldeans, her princes and wise men, her warriors and charioteers, her mercenaries, her treasures, and her discredited diviners. Each group is confronted with the sword; the result will be confusion (v. 36), destruction, failure of nerve, and plundering. Babylon as a nation will resemble a parched land. The land will be forsaken and become the habitat of wild beasts. A prose verse ends the poem with the future comparison of Babylon's destruction with that of the cities overthrown by Yahweh in the days of Sodom and Gomorrah (v. 40).

The Foe from the North (50:41-46)

An oracle quite parallel to 6:22-24 warns Babylon of the foe from the north; it is a force of many kings from afar and a great nation, who with cavalry and bowmen will attack Babylon savagely. The news will overwhelm the king with anguish.

This oracle (vv. 44-46) is duplicated in 49:17-21, with this difference; there it is applied to Edom, here, to Babylon. For analysis see 49:17 ff. in the commentary.

The Imminent Doom of Babylon (51:1-5)

This is the beginning of the second major oracle against Babylon in chapter 51. Yahweh announced that he is stirring up a foe against Babylon to winnow the land in a day of trouble. The might of the attackers renders resistance useless (v. 3), as the inhabitants of Babylon are victimized by the foe. The justification for this assault on Babylon derives from her guilt against Yahweh and from their enslavement of Israel and Judah, who despite appearances have not been overlooked by Yahweh.

The Guilt and Fall of Babylon (51:6-10)

The Babylonians are urgently admonished to flee from Babylon to save their lives and not be caught in the divine visitation of Yahweh's vengeance. Babylon had once been a golden cup, authenticated at that juncture of history by Yahweh's permission; she made the nations drunk with her wine (compare 25:15 ff.). But now Babylon has been broken; she is a fit subject for lamentation. Her illness was serious; now it is terminal. She might have survived, but now she is incurable (v. 9). The verse suggests that Babylon might have survived as a nation if she had enshrined enduring principles of

righteousness in her regime. While here and there the harshness of
the Babylonian captivity is mentioned (Isa. 47:6; 14:17; Jer. 50:33),
the ruling monarch Nebuchadnezzar is thrice referred to as the
servant of Yahweh (25:9; 27:6; 43:10), and Babylon was chosen as the
land wherein Judah would be revived; but such positive notes were
overshadowed by the sinister, and judgment was ripe for the nation.
Let all who seek safety, then, forsake Babylon.

The Governance of Yahweh (51:11-19)

Again comes the tone of war, the command to prepare for
encounter. It would seem the injunction is directed to the Median
attackers as they unknowingly become the instruments of Yahweh,
to take vengeance on the Babylonians for the destruction of the
Jerusalem Temple (compare 50:28). The Medes are urged to invade
Babylon with watchmen and ambushes; in so doing they would
fulfill the purpose of Yahweh in regard to Babylon. A brief lament
follows in which Babylon, which dwelt by many waters, so rich in
treasures, is pictured as having come to her sad end amid the
multitudinous foe who raise cries of victory over her. Verses 14-19
are repeated from 10:12-16 and like Isaiah 40—66 (compare Isa.
40:18 ff.), contrast in hymnic style the Almighty Creator, Yahweh of
hosts, the portion of Jacob, with the vain, worthless, and delusive
idols of Babylon.

The Hammer of Yahweh (51:20-24)

Who the "Hammer" was is doubtful. Is it, as seems most likely,
the Babylonian power (compare 27:6; 50:23) or some other power? If
it is Babylon, the poem describes how Yahweh used this nation to
accomplish his purpose. All classes of society are involved in the
fracture that Yahweh is accomplishing. Babylon with its irresistible
might once ruled without peer. Now the situation is rudely reversed, and Babylon is to be broken. In verse 24, following the
martial ode, the solemn words are recorded that Yahweh would
require of the Babylonians recompense for the evil that they had
done to Zion.

Confrontation of Babylon by Yahweh (51:25-26)

The oracle presents the challenging words of Yahweh in opposition to the destroying mountain (Babylon) which had destroyed the

whole earth. Yahweh would so devastate the mountain (Babylon) that no stone will be of size to become a foundation; indeed, the whole will be a perpetual waste.

The Call to Fading Colors (51:27-33)

The poem is concerned with the siege and destruction of Babylon. It begins with a call to the colors of nations hostile to Babylon. The northern nations of Ararat (Urartu), Minni (Mannai), and Ashkenaz (Ashguzai in the Lake Van region) are bidden to prepare war against Babylon. Likewise the kings of the Medes and their dependents are readying themselves for an attack against Babylon. The vast coalition of the foe, raised up to fulfill Yahweh's designs, inspires terror in the hearts of the Babylonians. They are paralyzed by fear as the houses of the city are fired and the bars of her gates are broken. Communiqués to the king of Babylon indicate siege on every side, with his soldiers deserting at the prospect. And Babylon will become like a threshing floor in time of harvest (compare Amos 8:1 ff.).

An Imprecatory Psalm (51:34-40)

Israel lamented that Nebuchadnezzar had devoured the nation with unspeakable violence and uttered a curse that Babylon be responsible for that guilt. To place blood upon others means to pay them back with judgment. Such is the word that Jerusalem uttered against Babylon. The petition was heard; Yahweh adopted the cause and took vengeance upon Babylon. With her vitality sapped and her land a heap of ruins, Babylon would experience recompense for her hurt to Judah. Though she roar like a lion, yet she would be like one deeply intoxicated. Disaster shall befall her without her awakening, and she will be brought to her slaughter as a dumb beast.

A Dirge Over Babylon (51:41-44)

This is a lament over Babylon, the praise of the whole earth, which had now been taken by her enemies. As the engulfing sea with its tumultuous waves, the Babylonian cities would become a revolting sight without inhabitant, a veritable desert. Her god Bel is in like predicament and will have to "cough up" his ill-gotten food; that is, his upkeep—fame, riches, and power—will be taken from him, and nations shall no longer flow to his worship when the walls of Babylon have fallen.

Israel's Release, Babylon's Fall (51:45-49)

The poem encourages Israel to flee from Babylon to overcome the fearful disaster now unfolding in Babylon, where violence and treason are abroad in the land. One can only imagine the mixed emotions that surged through the Judean captives as they witnessed the disintegration of the Babylonian power. Yahweh had promised that the idols of Babylon would be punished (discredited) and her shame and her slain would be enormous. Then, when Babylon falls, universal rejoicing will break forth, as the foe from the north victoriously vanquishes Babylon.

An Oracle of Encouragement (51:50-51)

The exiles in Babylon were encouraged to make their journey toward Jerusalem, despite the fact that aliens had profaned the Temple, involving Israel in national shame. The tedious journey from Babylon to Judah, the dangers of unpoliced highways, particularly now that Babylon's authority was diverted elsewhere, the discouraging prospect that awaited the returnees in Palestine—all these needed to be viewed and overcome with encouragement and resoluteness now that Babylon was on the verge of disintegration.

The Judgment of Babylon (51:52-53)

Here is another oracle forecasting the doom of Babylonian idolatry. Even though it had enjoyed prestige and power, destroyers from Yahweh would lay it low with the groans of her wounded devotees throughout the land.

The Destroyer Destroyed (51:54-58)

It is Yahweh who was laying Babylon waste, stilling her mighty voice, and cutting short her stormy activity. The defending warriors are captured; their bows are broken in pieces. They will be like drunken men. Strange, unbelievable, weird will be the reality before them, yet real, for Yahweh would make them drunk; princes, wisemen, rulers, and the military would sleep the eternal sleep, said Yahweh of hosts, the King. Verse 57 is repeated from verse 39.

The final oracle (v. 58) foresees the broad wall of Babylon leveled to the ground, her high gates burned with fire, the people and the nations laboring wearily for nothing—a sentiment that a loyal Yahwist would utter as he divined that beneath the facade of history

was the Lord of hosts and that all efforts contrary to his purpose
were vanity and weariness.

The Book of Babylon by Jeremiah (51:59-64).

In this biographical notice Jeremiah entrusted to Seraiah the
quartermaster, who was about to be deported with Zedekiah to
Babylon in 586 BC, a book containing all the prophecies of doom
relating to the downfall of Babylon. He instructed him further that
when he arrived in Babylon, Seraiah was to read all the book to the
exiles, and recite a prayer reminding Yahweh of his purposes
regarding the judgment of Babylon. Then Seraiah was to bind a
stone to the book, cast it into the Euphrates, and say, "Thus shall
Babylon sink, to rise no more, because of the evil that I (Yahweh) am
bringing upon her." The historical recital then concluded with the
words: "Thus far are the words of Jeremiah."

The length of the two compositions (chs. 50—51) indicates the
importance of the theme: the overthrow of Babylon. The extent of
the Babylonian oracles compares favorably with the attention given
this nation in Isaiah 13—14. The oracles affirm a number of general
statements of faith of the ardent Yahwists: (1) that Judah/Israel will
return to the Promised Land; (2) that the returning exiles will be a
regenerated people, purged of their idolatries; (3) that the Davidic
kingdom will be restored; and (4) that Yahweh will bring destruction
upon the heathen nations.

The Historical Appendix
52:1-34

The editor of the Book of Isaiah inserted from the Book of 2 Kings
(18:13 to 20:19) materials that now occupy chapters 36—39 in the
Book of Isaiah with the exception of Isaiah 38:9-20, a thanksgiving
psalm of Hezekiah. The apparent reason for this was to give the
readers of the scroll of Isaiah 1—35 an understanding of the writer,
which the historical background alone could provide. For a similar
reason, and from the same source (2 Kings 24:18 to 25:30), the editor
of the Book of Jeremiah concluded with the relevant historical

information necessary for the reader's understanding. The Book of Jeremiah is further enriched by the excellent historical materials included in chapters 39:1-10 and 40:7 to 43:7.

The Reign of Zedekiah (52:1-11)

With the four normal formulas used in introducing the Judean kings after the fall of Samaria, Zedekiah is presented: (1) his age at accession: twenty-one; (2) the length of his reign: eleven years; (3) his mother's name: Hamutal, the daughter of Jeremiah of Libnah—no relation to the prophet Jeremiah; and (4) a critique of his reign: evil like Jehoiakim's and responsible for the fall of Jerusalem.

In the ninth year of his reign (January, 588 BC) Nebuchadnezzar besieged Jerusalem, a siege that lasted until the eleventh year of Zedekiah (August, 587 BC). The beginning of the end was in sight when the food supply was exhausted. Rather than be captured by the Babylonians, Zedekiah and some military associates attempted to escape by night to Ammon; but they were apprehended by the Chaldeans in the plains of Jericho. Without his army, Zedekiah was brought before Nebuchadnezzar at Riblah where the war crimes were being judged. He was blinded after he had witnessed the slaughter of his sons. The royal princes were likewise killed while Zedekiah was bound and imprisoned in Babylon until he died.

The Destruction of the Temple (52:12-27)

In the fifth month (August, 587 BC) Nebuzaradan entered Jerusalem and burned the Temple and the houses in the city. He broke down the walls around Jerusalem. Then he assembled those scheduled for deportation. These were numbered from the upper classes of the people and the survivors of the Jerusalem seizure together with the Judeans who had deserted to the Babylonians. However, he did leave some of the poorest of the land to be vinedressers and plowmen, to prevent the land from returning to its wild state. From the Temple itself the Chaldeans transported to Babylon the vessels of service and the furniture, an act which is described in pathetic, nostalgic terms. Then Nebuzaradan took from among the Judeans some prominent Temple officials, the military commander in charge of Jerusalem, seven men of the royal council, the secretary of the commander of the army who enlisted the people of the land, and sixty men of the rural areas. These were transported to Riblah and executed (vv. 24-27).

The Judean Captivities (52:28-30)

This is a statement of the time and number of the captivities Judah suffered. The first was in 597 BC when Jehoiachin surrendered in the seventh year of Nebuchadnezzar, involving some 3,023 captives (2 Kings 24:12-16). The second was in 587 BC, the eighteenth year of Nebuchadnezzar, involving some 832 captives; and the third occurred in 582 BC (compare 40:7 to 41:18; 2 Kings 14:22-26) in the twenty-third year of Nebuchadnezzar and involved 745 exiles. The total number of Judeans that were led into exile is therefore 4,600. This is a very small number, to be sure, but these would serve as hostages of the Jews elsewhere, particularly those in Palestine. They would represent also the intelligentsia, without whom future rebellion would not be likely.

The Release of Jehoiachin (52:31-34)

The Book of Jeremiah concludes with the notice of the release of Jehoiachin from his Babylonian imprisonment by Amel-marduk (biblical: Evil-merodach) after thirty-seven years. The deposed Judean monarch was treated graciously, shown preference over other hostage kings, and allotted provision from the king for his daily needs until he died.

LAMENTATIONS

Introduction

Title and Place in Canon

The Book of Lamentations is known as *How!* in the Hebrew Bible and derives that title from the early custom of naming a composition by the introductory word(s). The word itself is an interrogative adverb commonly used as the initial word of a dirge (funeral song). The Greek translation of the Old Testament about 200 BC translated the term with "lamentations," from which the Latin and the English titles proceed. The name of the book was also called *dirges* in the Talmud (*Baba bathra* 14*b*,15*a*). This latter term described in general the contents of the book and, more particularly, identified the writings as compositions that generally conform to the *qinah* poetic metrical type, a 3 + 2 rhythm, in which the second half of the line lacks one third of the first part of the line. This type of poetic meter was used extensively in the dirges or lamentations for the dead.

In the Hebrew Bible, the Book of Lamentations is the fourth book of the *Scrolls*, which occupy the fourth to the ninth places in the third division of the Hebrew Bible known as the Writings (compare Luke 24:44, where "psalms . . ." being the first book in the third division gives the name to the entire third collection). In the Greek, Latin, and English Bibles the book follows immediately after the Book of Jeremiah. This location was accorded the book because of the supposed authorship of Jeremiah.

Authorship and Date

There is a persistent tradition that the Book of Lamentations was composed by Jeremiah. Support for this opinion has been sought in 2 Chronicles 35:24-25, where the national mourning for the beloved King Josiah is described: "All Jerusalem mourned for Josiah. Jeremiah also uttered a lament . . .; behold, they are written in the Laments." In the Greek Bible there is an introduction provided which is lacking in the Hebrew. It reads:

And it came to pass after Israel was taken captive, and Jerusalem made desolate, that Jeremiah sat weeping, and lamented with this lamentation over Jerusalem, and said;

then follows Lamentations 1:1.

The first quotation hardly bears out the contention that Jeremiah wrote the Book of Lamentations. Josiah was slain in 609 BC, some twenty years before the events mentioned in Lamentations occurred. Male and female lamenters were held in singular high esteem in Judean society as indispensable personnel in the mourning ceremonies for the dead, and they had no doubt their repertoire of dirges. However, it does not follow that Jeremiah wrote anything other than a personal lament for his revered monarch.

The second quotation is a divergent tradition from the Hebrew Bible and must be viewed as originating centuries after the Book of Lamentations was canonized. Accordingly, it has little value in determining the authorship of the book.

There is no easy solution. The internal evidence upon which the question must be evaluated has been viewed as supporting the authorship of Jeremiah as well as suggesting a non-Jeremianic composition.

Alleged evidence for the authorship of Jeremiah includes the above two quotations, the striking similarities between Jeremiah's grief and Lamentations 3, the poetic ability of the writer and the deeply moving two line poems (couplets) throughout the entire book. All of these indicate some temperamental affinity: their shared theological posture in attributing the destruction of Jerusalem to the sins of Judah; the fact that the writer must have been an eyewitness of the events surrounding Jerusalem's fall; and many interesting parallel phrases and similarities of style. On the other hand, it has been argued that the alphabetic style of Lamentations is quite foreign from the poetic compositions of Jeremiah, that the theological pronouncements of Jeremiah are quite different than Lamentations in a number of important issues (compare 4:17 with Jer. 37:5-10, where the former suggests a Judean dependence on Egypt; or 4:20 with Jer. 24:8-10, where the former supports Zedekiah), and other important considerations presented fully in S.R. Driver's *Introduction to the Old Testament*. The authorship cannot be settled with any degree of certainty, and most scholars leave the question undecided. But certain affirmations can be made about the author(s) when one reviews the data of the book itself.

The data about the authorship indicate the following about the writer or writers (and most scholars tend toward a unity of authorship if for no other reason than the arguments advocating a plurality of contributors are less convincing). The writer must certainly have been an eyewitness of the sorrowful years when Judah was being enslaved by the Babylonians and a resident within Jerusalem during its final siege, when the suffering from famine, disease, militarism, and terror all impressed his sensitive nature and found expression in his profoundly moving poetry. While much of the Old Testament is anonymous, the writer must have been a singularly gifted poet equal to, if not identical with, Jeremiah, for Lamentations, in spite of its alphabetic limitations, is one of the profoundest lyrical analyses of human tragedy and one of the most articulate collection of dirges ever penned. To its author all subsequent generations owe an immense debt for his poetic, lyric, psychological, and religious contribution.

It would seem from the internal evidence of the book itself that the five compositions all date from the period after the capture of Jerusalem in 586 BC. Chapter 5 embraces a historical and political setting somewhat later than the other chapters and depicts the exceedingly difficult days the Judean remnant had to endure under the firmly entrenched Babylonian provincial government. A date of 570 BC would be appropriate.

Literary Structure

The first four chapters of Lamentations are alphabetic compositions (termed by some acrostic). Chapters 1 and 2 have twenty-two verses, each verse having three lines. The first line of each verse in these two chapters uses a letter of the Hebrew alphabet, beginning with the first letter and continuing to the last letter. In chapter 3 there are also twenty-two verses, each with three lines, but here every line in each verse has the appropriate letter of the Hebrew alphabet. Thus verse 1 has three lines each beginning with the first letter, verse 2 has three lines each beginning with the second letter, and so on. Chapter 4 has twenty-two verses but only forty-four lines; in this composition the first line of each verse has the proper letter of the alphabet, similar to chapters 1 and 2. In chapter 5 the alphabetic form is dropped, but the length of the composition with its twenty-two verses and twenty-two lines agrees at least with the number of Hebrew letters. Accordingly, we have verses with three lines (chs. 1,

2, and 3), verses with two lines (ch. 4), and verses of only one line (ch. 5). In chapters 2, 3, and 4 the seventeenth letter is exchanged with the sixteenth letter.

The use of the alphabet in sophisticated poetry appears strange to the modern reader, but its presence in the Old Testament is witnessed in Psalms 9—10,25,34,37,111—112,119 (this last like Lam. 3, but with eight lines in each stanza), 145, Proverbs 31:10-31, and in Nahum 1:2-10*b* (incomplete). The alphabet and numbers appear to have been used as an aid to memory (compare Prov. 30:15-33). It has been suggested that in using the alphabet the writer was attempting to suggest that the composition is all inclusive, from "A" to "Z" (compare Rev. 1:8,11; 21:6; 22:13).

The literary types involved in the Book of Lamentations are generally agreed upon by modern scholars, but some discussion must be undertaken to clarify the underlying problems. Among the literary forms in the general area of the lament are the dirges. Such compositions are discoverable in the Old Testament as in the dirge of David over Saul and Jonathan (2 Sam. 1:17-27, where the typical exclamation, *How!* appears three times: vv. 19,25,27) and his lament over Abner (2 Sam. 3:32 ff.). The use of the dirge was expanded in literary use to convey in the most solemn form the immediate death of a nation. Amos used the dirge most effectively in Amos 5:1 and following, where in the characteristic *qinah* meter he lamented the death of Israel (compare Jer. 7:29; 9:17-22; Ezek. 19).

There are other laments which effectively express the grief and emotion of a community (city or state) or of an individual. The first type, the communal psalm of lament, is a psalm lamenting the ravaging of a foe, a plague, a famine, or some other national disaster. The people assembled at the house of God, offered fitting sacrifices, and poured out their complaints of woe and their earnest prayers for the betterment of the distressing situation. Often the people made national vows as a convincing proof of their sincerity and anticipated the divine help with an anticipatory thanksgiving psalm. Naturally the voice is that of the community, the "we" of the suppliants; or, when it is "I," it is the corporate "I," with the solo voice speaking for the entire community. Such communal laments are well represented throughout the entire Old Testament, particularly in the Psalter (for example, Pss. 44, 74, 79, 80, 83).

The individual psalm of lamentation is normally occasioned when personal woes have befallen the lamenter, such as sickness, misfortune, hostile plottings of his enemies, and numerous other calamities. The composition usually begins with a very abbreviated prayer or a reproachful question (compare Ps. 22), then plunges into the lament in which the person praying described his various problems in general terms. The prayer follows, largely in keeping with his difficulties expressed in the description of distress. The prayer often shows the suppliant rising in courage and faith to such an extent that he envisions the better future with joyful thanksgiving. Thus Psalm 22 which begins with the words "My God, my God, why . . .?" ends with a thanksgiving composition (vv. 22-31).

The thanksgiving composition borrows from another category of psalms, the individual/communal thanksgiving composition. It is less animated than the hymn but does begin with some type of praise formula. There follows a description of the distress from which the individual was rescued. The psalmist tells how in despair he had cried unto Yahweh and was heard and delivered from all his woes (compare Ps. 32:5; 34:4; 40:1 ff.). Now having completed the story of his calamities, the psalmist gives thanks, offers testimony of his experience, and invites others to permit Yahweh to do for them what he has done for the psalmist. Such thanksgiving, personal testimony, and moralization of the experience of salvation secure for themselves a large portion in the individual and communal psalms of lamentation. The basic difference between the communal and individual psalm of lamentation is that the former is voiced by the community while the latter is recited by the individual as a personal experience.

It would appear that Lamentations 1, 2, 4, and 5 are communal laments, perhaps with overtones of dirge motifs, while chapter 3 resembles an individual psalm of lamentation where the individual, nonetheless, represents the community.

Importance of the Book of Lamentations

Historical Importance.—This half century (ca. 609-550 BC) including the fall of Judah constitutes one of the most important eras in the history of Israel, and, happily, it is more fully documented than any other period in the nation's history. Supplementing the historical recitals in 2 Kings and 2 Chronicles, the prophets have detailed the fortunes, personages, and events that transpired before their very eyes. Zephaniah and Habakkuk introduced the themes and the events of this half century; Jeremiah was the keen observer and critical analyst in Jerusalem; Isaiah 40—66 and the writings of Ezekiel were penned on location in Babylon; Obadiah records the hateful arrogance of faithless Edom in the disastrous years of Jerusalem's fall (587-86 BC). The products of these prophets combine to furnish us with historical reports and critiques of national policy, sociological inequities, and character deficiencies.

The Book of Lamentations zeros in on the events of the fall of Jerusalem to describe in unforgettable vividness the inescapable might of the Babylonian oppression; the utter pathos of the various strata of society as they succumbed to the horrors of the final capture: famine, disease, and unconquerable terror; and the bankruptcy of their formerly optimistic religious affirmations, as more and more they felt frustrated, fearful, betrayed, deserted by their leaders and God. Lamentations provides a lyric depth to the dark days of the siege. Sensitive readers of the book feel empathetic toward the wretched participants in this tragic drama.

Cultural Importance.—Crises evoke a literary productivity seldom witnessed in peaceful times. The challenge-response syndrome is particularly evident in the communal tragedies of a nation. When the foundations are shaken, people are exercised to find enduring values and meaningfulness that will interpret the fragmentation they are called upon to endure. Without the religious tensions of a society harassed from without and within, the creative drive would have escaped the prophets and the sages, leaving the world impoverished by their silence. In the climax of suffering, when hope had vanished, when the darkness settled in, the redemptive light was seen and given expression. Such was the backdrop of the Lamentations, one of the finest periods of poetic activity in the long history of Israel. Lamentations was born in that time of suffering.

With its eyewitness truth and equal emotion, with its variety of literary patterns, with its deft strokes and admirable movement, with its timing proper to its report, the book has enriched the categories of world laments; but, more particularly, it has portrayed one of the noblest experiences in the human drama: a hopeless, beaten, frustrated people directing their hearts in pitiful lament to their God. The curtain descends; there is no divine help indicated, no sudden solution to rectify the wrongs. Nothing occupies the stage except the tears of the bewildered which alone he commends to God—no words, no suggestions, just a prostrate form with head bowed to the ground! The curtain closes; the lights fade into darkness; the book is ended. This is authentic life.

The poetic, the dramatic, the literary genius of Lamentations has given it a preeminent place in the literature of the world. It is tragic that the book is so little used in the church at large, so circumscribed in the lessons or the responsive readings, so seldom read, and so seldom appreciated. It deserves a greater reading audience as a literary classic unexcelled in the Hebrew Scriptures.

Religious Importance.—This theme has been hinted at previously; it now remains to discuss its theological significance more particularly.

It has been proposed that the Book of Lamentations addresses itself to the problem of how God can be good and allow the evil of the Babylonian conquest to happen to Judah. Granted that the Judeans had fallen short in ethical achievement and were justly subject to the divine judgment, the writer, in this view, labors to maintain that the people of Judah have suffered through the Babylonians far beyond any semblance of justice. Was it not discriminatory that Babylonians should succeed and Yahweh's people suffer (compare Hab. 1)? The question certainly must have been raised. Here and there in Lamentations the problem is seen; but the purpose of the book is larger than a treatise on a good God and the existence of evil however important that might be.

It has been suggested that the purpose of the book should be sought along other lines. The Temple in Jerusalem was conceived to be the sacred abode of Yahweh; it had stood since the days of Solomon. No foreign foe had successfully threatened it. When Sennacherib attempted to capture Jerusalem in the days of Isaiah, he suffered an embarrassing disappointment. Accordingly, it was widely held that Zion could not be taken and that the Temple of Yahweh would abide forever. But, shockingly, the Babylonians entered the city, carried off the sacred furniture, and burned the Temple without any divine deterrent. The Book of Lamentations, therefore, has been considered to be an attempt to explore how this could have happened and to formulate a solution to the embarrassing dilemma. No doubt, this popular faith contributed to the problem of the Judean disaster in the sixth century, but it is only one aspect of the larger perplexity.

The religious importance of the Book of Lamentations may be formulated in a series of propositions, not necessarily presented in the order of their importance, but whose inclusion in the discussion will provide a more substantial foundation.

1. The Book of Lamentations provides a portrait of that most significant period in which are depicted the divine and human elements as they confronted one another. It was a period of intense suffering, a time when a multiform religious experience developed, a time of rebellion; it was a period of contrition, penitence, and resolution.

2. The Book of Lamentations provides a mirror for the subsequent generations, a touchstone to evaluate essential religion, and an admonition to avoid those devious practices which occasioned the tragic fall of Jerusalem. The five poems were eminently useful in the creative liturgy of the Exilic period and must have been incorporated almost immediately into the laments chanted in the fast liturgies (Zech. 7:3,5; 8:19; Esther 4:3 ff.; 9:31).

The momentous events that surrounded the Babylonian capture of Judah furnished the themes and the calendar for the Exilic fasts: the siege of Jerusalem, observed on the tenth day of the tenth month (2 Kings 25:1; Jer. 52:4; Zech. 8:19); the breach in the walls of Jerusalem, celebrated on the ninth day of the fourth month (Zech 8:19; compare Jer. 39:2; 52:6-8; 2 Kings 25:3-5); the burning of the city, observed on the tenth day of the fifth month (2 Kings 25:8; Zech. 7:3 ff.; 8:19); and the assassination of Gedaliah, observed on the third or the twenty-fourth day of the seventh month (2 Kings 25:23 ff.; Jer. 41:1 ff.). In the Jewish community the Book of Lamentations has been read in observance of the destruction of Jerusalem, no doubt beginning in the Exilic period and continuing to the present on the ninth day of the fifth month. After the destruction of the Temple in AD 70, the Jews observed both destructions of the city on the ninth day of the fifth month and read the Book of Lamentations as a fitting Scripture for the occasion. All this indicates how deep an impression was made upon the Judeans by this mind-shattering disaster, and the reading of the Lamentations reprints on the Jewish consciousness the solemn lessons so tragically depicted therein. The book added a significant dimension and contribution to the liturgy of Judaism.

3. The Book of Lamentations is a descriptive recital of tragedy. Looking at this tragedy produces varying responses from the viewer. While these reactions differ considerably, there appears to be in the pathetic portrayal one essential question, and this appears to be the purpose of the book. That question poses the persistent interroga-

tive Why? What is the purpose of the tragedy? Do we not possess the land? Is the city not rightfully ours? Why do foreigners torment us with their insatiable greed to rob us of our city, our possessions, our freedom? What purpose can there be in life? Is it to become slaves? Why is it that we who have named Yahweh as our God, however imperfectly we have followed him, should now be starving for food, terrified by fear, and possessed of no hope? For tomorrow is the slave camp, the Exile into an accursed enemy's land, to be his chattel, to see our land no more, to lose our children, to be subjected to all the indignities of captivity. Lamentations does not propose any solutions, save here and there an imprecatory wish to curse the enemy; the lamenter was too crushed by his woe to imagine that he had any worthy solution to the problem.

It is when the book is read in the great pessimism of the events that the essential problem surfaces. That problem appears to this writer to be: What is the meaning of life, this kind of life, which time, weakness, and destiny have meted out for us? It is the problem of Victor Frankl at Auschwitz, the problem of Rabbi Kushner of New England. Is there life in tragedy; is there meaningfulness in apparent hopelessness? The book suggests to the reader no simple resolution; it does, however, create the impression of something significant when everything is chaos. It suggests that in Auschwitz life is to be found, even if it be for the moment when one shares one's precious crust of bread with one just lately gone berserk. It is found at Walden Pond where Thoreau "did not wish to live what was not life." Life must not be confused with livelihood. Man does not live by bread alone; nor is one's life the abundance of things one possesses.

By millions confessed, the greatest hour in human history was when one, amid the degradation of a cross and afflicted with pain, reached out in those fleeting moments to others, exhibited what possibility was in tragedy, changed torment to triumph, and chose as his memorial symbol a redeeming cross.

The sorrowful hour portrayed in the Book of Lamentations may appear quite hopeless and forlorn, but it contained the possibility that the tragedy could mean something. That something was realized by the Exilic community, and those that followed after, to give meaning to Israel and her mission throughout the world.

The meaning of the Book of Lamentations is not stated. Its influence upon its readers discloses its importance and its message.

Chapter 1

This alphabetically arranged lament consists of twenty-two verses; each verse has three lines, the first of which begins with a different letter of the Hebrew alphabet, beginning with the first letter and proceeding to the last letter. The structure of the composition clearly indicates two divisions: vv. 1-11 and vv. 12-22. Each part has its individualistic approach.

The Description of Distress (1:1-11)

Jerusalem appears first upon the stage as "the city" (vv. 1-2), then as "Judah" (v. 3), to be followed by "Zion" (vv. 4-6) and finally "Jerusalem" (vv. 7-11*b*). The city is described in the third person, singular, feminine. As the subject shifts from one designation to another, the minor characters who articulate the description and the backdrops come into focus as the theme of the disaster of Jerusalem is projected.

The lonely city (vv. 1-2).—Contrasts between the glorious past and the dismal present constitute both a temporal and qualitative comparison and are often utilized very effectively in the structure of the lamentation (compare Pss. 44:1-16; 74:2 ff.; 80:4-13). The city is pictured presently as sitting alone, whereas once she was populous. Now she is a "widow," whereas once she was "great among the nations." Once she was a "princess"; now she is a "vassal." Having had all, it is harder to fall to nothing at all.

The metaphor changes to picture Jerusalem as a woman weeping bitterly with a profusion of tears upon her cheeks, persistently inconsolable into the night. All her lovers (political allies) afford no comfort; all her friends (lovers, political allies) have deceitfully dealt with her and have become her enemies (compare the treachery of Edom: Jer. 27:3 with Obad. 10-14).

Exiled Judah (v. 3).—The poet deplores the sorry state of the Judeans. In the portrayal of the forlorn, homeless exiles in the strange land of Babylon, the poet indicated their restive spirit and the unbearable distress which their pursuers have now forced upon the captives. Hopelessness and homesickness, fear of the unknown, longing for the old and familiar sight, and grieving for the dead were unconsolable hardships the survivors of Judah now had to endure.

The dirge of Zion (vv. 4-7).—The first facet of this section is the lack of worshipers frequenting the ways to Zion; the appointed feasts are now unattended. The gates of Zion, once filled with feasting and life, are now deserted. The priests groan at the new and strange way of life. Maidens are seduced and ravished. Jerusalem is a disaster area from every vantage point; Zion suffers bitterly from the tragic situation.

The second theme bewailed is that the foes of Zion have become the prosperous heads of the new Judean regime, a plight occasioned by the judgment of Yahweh upon the national sin. The hope of the nation, the youth of Zion, have departed; they are prisoners of war in the hand of the enemy (v. 5).

The third component concerns the departed majesty of Zion. Her princes resemble hounded harts exhausted in the chase before the pursuer (v. 6). The final aspect of distress is the contrast between the present days of dire affliction and bitterness and the former days of affluence and comfort so long enjoyed (v. 7), days which even Yahweh remembered! These are gone forever since Judah succumbed to the foe without any supportive hand to assist. The foe gloated and mocked at her downfall (compare 4:16; Obad. 11-13). This mocking tried their souls, but nothing could be done except to bear it.

Jerusalem undone by her deeds (vv. 8-11).—The poet frankly admitted the national sin of Judah and likened it to the sinful ways of a woman of the streets. The city that had attracted so many had become repulsive now to her imagined friends; indeed, she was overcome with her own vileness. Impurity reigned in her life but she was oblivious to the judgment it would bring until her terrible fall. Now, without comforter, she pleaded with Yahweh to look upon her affliction which the triumphant enemy had inflicted (v. 9).

The enemy had made off with all the precious things of Jerusalem (compare Jer. 52:17-23). Even the Temple had been violated by the heathen nations forcing entry into the sacred precincts (v. 10). The starving people groan as they forage for food and trade their treasures for the more precious bread (v. 11).

The first half of the lament ends with Jerusalem herself speaking in the first person and addressing a prayer to Yahweh for compassion, similar to the plea in 1:9*b*. Both of these prayers are buttressed by motivation clauses, pleading with Yahweh to fulfill the request because of the triumph of the enemy (v. 9) and the insufferable disdain of the enemy (v. 11*c*).

The Lamentation, Part II (1:12-22)

The change from the third person feminine singular in 1:1-11 to the first person singular in 1:12-22, together with the replacement of such terms for Jerusalem as "city" (v. 1), "Judah" (v. 3), "Zion" (vv. 4,6), and "Jerusalem" (vv. 7-8) with the first person singular, permits the poet, speaking in the name of Jerusalem, a greater freedom and personal identity. It is the corporate "I" of the community speaking as though it were an individual. The change in person was forecast in the two prayers in verses 9 and 11c.

The lament begins its new phase by petitioning the travelers who pass by the ruined city to behold the enormity of the tragedy and to respond to two queries: Does what you see mean anything to you? and Have you ever seen such sorrow as mine? These are rhetorical questions designed to emphasize the intensity of the disaster by eliciting sympathy from the wayfarers and asking them to evaluate comparatively the sorrow of Jerusalem with the sorrow witnessed elsewhere in their journeys.

The sorrows ("these things," v. 16) are then depicted under several diverse guises (vv. 13-15). The woes are attributed directly to Yahweh who, in his fierce anger, has inflicted them upon Jerusalem and are presented under the following figures: (1) sickness/fever: "He sent fire; into my bones he made it descend" (v. 13a); (2) a trapper's net: "he spread a net for my feet" (v. 13b), a rejection which left the city stunned and without strength; (3) an oppressive yoke: transgressions were bound into a yoke, fastened together, and set upon the neck with resultant weakness (v. 14); (4) surrender: Yahweh gave me into the hand of the irresistible enemy (v. 14c); (5) scoffing: Yahweh treated the military defenders of Jerusalem with contempt (v. 15a); (6) banquet: Yahweh has called an assembly of guests whose dastardly purpose was to crush the Judeans; and joined with this is (7) wine press: Yahweh treads the wine press, crushing his beloved people and, so it would seem, providing thereby the wine for the assembled guests (v. 15; compare Zeph. 1:7 ff.; Ezek. 39:17-20; Isa. 63:1-6).

The reaction to such tragic events (v. 16) is unmitigated sorrow ("I weep; my eyes flow with tears"), an abysmal loneliness ("a comforter is far from me, one to revive my courage"), and bereavement ("my children are desolate"). The penitent then entreatingly stretched out her hand in vain, for there was none to comfort; instead Yahweh had

transformed the neighbors of Jacob into his foes, and Jerusalem had
become a filthy discard (v. 17).

Once again the confession of guilt was freely acknowledged
(v. 18a), but still the painful effects of its judgment dominated the
entire scene. The anguish was immediately spelled out in terms of
suffering, of maidens and young men in Exile, of faithless allies, of
priests and elders starving to death (v. 18 ff.). From the poignant
distress that troubles without, the poet refocuses upon the woes that
are within: distress, tumult, and the changing of the mind—all this
under a heavy burden of guilt (rebellion). Returning to the disasters,
the writer beholds death bereaving in the street and illness in the
house. The sorrow was intensified because it was endured alone.
There was no one to talk to, none to comfort. The enemies had
heard of the trouble; it had penetrated to their rank and file; and
they were glad that God had done it (v. 21).

The lamentation concludes with an imprecatory prayer:

> Bring thou the day thou hast announced;
>   and let them be as I am.
> Let all their evil-doing come before thee;
>   and deal with them
> as thou hast dealt with me (vv. 21b-22a).

The poet freely acknowledged that Yahweh had dealt with Jerusalem
in accordance with all her transgressions but prayed that Yahweh
would deal similarly with those who gloated over the misfortunes
Jerusalem and her people had suffered. Verse 22 ends in a motivation clause, "for my groans are many/and my heart is faint"; therefore the poet asked the Lord to deal with the enemies, the immediate cause of all the woes.

In reviewing this first lament there are five major themes to be
observed: (1) the heartrending devastation of Jerusalem and her
people; (2) the cause of the disaster, boldly identified as Yahweh.
Babylon (not mentioned by name in the lament) is the nearest
cause. (3) The moral reason for the disaster, conceived to be a divine
judgment and not political power, was the flagrant sin of Judah. (4)
Another theme is the spontaneous, frank, and honest confession of
Judah to have sinned against Yahweh and to be rightly answerable to
the judgment of God. This openhearted admission of the Exilic
community stands in sharp relief against the hypocritical and

pretentious confession of the monarchical period in Judah. (5) The prayers (vv. 9*c*,11*c*,20*a*,22) complete this list. The two prayers in the Revised Standard Version of verse 21 are better understood as in the past tense, following the Hebrew text.

There is an interesting problem raised when one considers the imprecatory prayer of verse 22. If Yahweh is determined to judge Jerusalem and has selected the Babylonians to fulfill this task, how may Israel then ask Yahweh to punish his servant (Babylon) when that agent was simply fulfilling the purpose of Yahweh? The general approach to the question is that Yahweh will not punish his servant for doing his will but for exceeding the divine order (compare Isa. 10:5-15).

Chapter 2

Beginning as do chapters 1 and 4, this composition opens with the outcry of deep lament. The chapter may be divided in four sections, with noticeable shades of change in the first two parts. The first segment of this lament contains verses 1-10 and has for its theme the grievous judgment inflicted upon Judah by Yahweh. Yahweh is the subject of the sentences, expressed or implied, in the first eight verses, but in verses 9 and 10 there occurs a general shift in the subject; Yahweh, except in verse 9*b*, fades from the focus, and the reader is prepared for the change which will take place in the second part of the lament (vv. 11-17). Here the poet assumed the lead with a personal cry of grief in verse 11*a* and *b*, followed immediately by the cause: the starving children (vv. 11*c*-12). Another pathetic outbreak occurs in verse 13, as he became overwhelmed by the incomparable suffering of Jerusalem. This thesis is implemented by three groups: the prophets (v. 14), the wayfarers (v. 15), and the enemies (v. 16). The conclusion is presented in verse 17, a summary statement of Yahweh's judgment on his people through their foes.

In verses 18 and 19 the poet summoned Zion to seek Yahweh ardently and persistently, to pour out their hearts before him for the sake of the starving children in the famine-stricken land. The chapter concludes with a communal lament, with a reproachful question and pathetic and bold incriminations of the divine providence (vv. 20-22).

Yahweh's Consuming Judgment (2:1-10)

The poet, as the voice of the community, described the terrible punishment meted out by Yahweh against Judah. He built up the concept of the nation with great tenderness; but Judah was now a rough, tough iron-clad man of war; she was not referred to even as a woman. However, she once was the daughter (an endearing term) of Zion (vv. 1,4,8,10), or of Judah (vv. 2,5), or the virgin daughter of Zion (v. 13), or the daughter of Jerusalem (vv. 13,15)—nine instances in which there are overtones of feminine fragility and tenderness. It is against this mildness that the harshness of the judgment of Yahweh is shown.

In this portion of the lament the poet in bitterness of spirit described the disaster that befell Judah and, more specifically, Jerusalem and its inhabitants. With the eerie background of the darkness of a cloud, the fearful devastation of the land is depicted. The secular city comes first into focus. The splendor of Israel, the very footstool of Yahweh—unless this is interpreted to be the Temple (compare Pss. 99:5; 132:7)—the habitations, the strongholds, the palaces, in a word, the kingdom, has been subjected to ruthless devastation, with the implication that most of the buildings were destroyed; the ramparts, the city gates, the wall of Zion, and the bars of the gates have shared in the tumultuous overthrow of Judah and her inhabitants. A second aspect concerns the lamentable fate of the Temple (v. 7); the sanctuary itself with its altar had been desecrated by the heathen amid boisterous clamor. The services were at an end; the law (justice and its enforcement) was no longer observed. The poet concluded this portion by indicating the personnel that had endured the tragedy: king and nobility were in Exile; the prophets were discredited and had no divine word; the elders (city officials) and maidens, clad in appropriate mourning garb, sat mute upon the ground.

The Poet's Lament (2:11-17)

In verse 11 the poet broke out in personal lament, unable to contain his emotions as he viewed the tragic suffering of the starving children (vv. 11-12). Again, he came forward to ask two questions of Jerusalem for one specific purpose: What can he say? To what may he compare the distress Zion was experiencing? Both questions are asked in order to offer some possible solace in the vast calamity which the nation was suffering. The plight is then more particularly examined under three heads: (1) The prophets who have proved deceptive, who have not warned of the danger that engulfed Jerusalem—they are the enemies within; (2) the wayfarers who pass by the ruins of Judah, applaud and scoff, and with biting sarcasm ask, "Is this the city which was called the perfection of beauty, the joy of all the earth?" (compare Ps. 48:2); (3) the triumphant enemies who rub salt in the wounds; they rail and hiss, derisively proclaiming their victory and their uncontainable, joyful vindictiveness.

In verse 17 the judgment of Yahweh is summed up as the fulfillment of his purpose ordained long since. He had used the enemy to carry out his will and made them to rejoice over his people. Indeed, in verse 5 it was said that Yahweh seemed to have joined their enemies in the destruction of his people.

With the lament proper completed, the poet now energetically urged the defeated people to petition for the salvation of Yahweh (vv. 18-19), to pour out their hearts continually for the dire needs of the starving children. The prayer, which largely recapitulates the lament, is then placed in the mouth of the distressed Judeans (vv. 20-22). Like many such prayers offered in deepest adversity, it blamed God. Yahweh was asked to behold the glaring inconsistencies. Two reproachful questions then follow, the strongest possible assertion in the Hebrew language; for the reproachful question not merely asserts powerfully the distressing condition, but involves an answer to the question in which the inconsistency occurs (compare Ps. 22:1). The people asked Yahweh to look upon those with whom he had been dealing so brutally as to force cannibalism upon devoted mothers. The second query is equally potent: Is it consistent with your divine policy to permit priest and prophet to be slain in your sanctuary? Isn't there something wrong somewhere and shouldn't something be done immediately to rectify the situation? The prayer then added a further distressing point: death was everywhere, among youth and age, maidens and young men. They have been slaughtered without mercy and without divine reprisal, and you, O God, are responsible: "In the day of thy anger thou hast slain them, slaughtering without mercy" (v. 21). If this were uttered in unbelief, it was blasphemy; if in faith, it was the utmost expression of depression. Yahweh is implored to view one more horrible scene: Yahweh seemed to invite us to a festal gathering; it proved to be an orgy of blood and massacre; none escaped or survived; the little ones whom we bounced on our knee and brought up, the enemy ruthlessly destroyed (compare Ps. 137:7-9).

It is a prayer similar to those uttered in Auschwitz or Dachau; it admits of no intellectual answer. Nowhere in the Bible is the problem more poignantly insisted, nowhere more pathetically described. Now as then, the only approach in the maze of the tragic remains, "Lord, to whom shall we go? thou hast the words of eternal life" (John 6:68, KJV).

Chapter 3

The alphabetic structure of this chapter differs from chapters 1, 2, and 4 in that every line in every verse begins with the respective Hebrew letter. Also the seventeenth letter and the eighteenth letter are reversed, as they are in chapters 2 and 4.

The chapter may be divided into two compositions: Part 1 has the form of an individual psalm of lamentation with an introductory "description of distress" (vv. 1-18) followed by a prayer, affirmations of faith, and testimonial moralization (vv. 19-39). Part 2 is likewise an individual psalm of lament and follows a pattern similar to part 1, with a "description of distress" or lament (vv. 41-54) followed by a prayer, oracle, and a recital of deliverance until it concludes with an imprecatory prayer (vv. 55-66).

The Hebraic concept of corporate personality, in which one man represents the nation, and the nation one man, enables the poet to speak in his own person yet truly represent the distressed community. This change of person intensifies the presentation of the suffering; it is much more expressive in personal terms than in the neuter concepts of city, walls, buildings, and faceless, statistical, suffering people. The formula of the lament becomes more intensely relative and empathetic; thus the change from the corporate to the individual allows the poet the best of both expressions.

The Description of Distress, Part 1 (3:1-18)

In these verses the writer draws a pathetic picture of personal sufferings and employs a wide range of reference. What he included in his self-portrait was, of course, to be projected as the lamentable situation that prevailed in the entire Judean community. The afflictions he endured he attributed directly and immediately to

Yahweh, though he was careful not to include the divine name but to refer to God in the third person singular pronoun. Verse 18 is the only exception in this portion.

In the lament proper, the speaker identified himself as one who had seen affliction and had been under the rod of divine wrath (v. 1). Yahweh was then indicted for inflicting this harsh and unfeeling suffering upon the lamenter, the speaker for the Judean community (vv. 2-18). Included in the incrimination were such charges as: God had driven him into darkness, turned his hand upon him repeatedly and continually (v. 2 ff.), plagued him with illness, enclosed him within bitterness and tribulation, and made him to dwell in death's gloom (vv. 3-6). He had walled him about without possibility of escape, manacled him with heavy chains, had remained implacable, and subverted his way with formidable difficulties (vv. 7-9). God had become to the sufferer like a bear and a lion, tearing him as though he were prey; he had desolated him and used him as a target for his archery practice; the arrows had deeply penetrated within (vv. 10-13). By such sadistic maltreatment the sufferer had become the laughingstock of all people, the theme of their songs (v. 14). God had filled him with bitterness and wormwood (v. 15). In the gravel he groveled with sand in his mouth or cowered in the ashes (v. 16). He was without peace and had forgotten the meaning of happiness (v. 17). Whatever self-esteem he had, whatever hopes he entertained, both were long since departed. The climax is the pessimistic conclusion: "Gone is . . . my expectation from the Lord" (v. 18).

The Prayer, Affirmations of Faith, and Testimonial Moralization (3:19-39)

The description of distress had drained the hurts and sorrows from the distressed speaker (vv. 1-18). Talking about his hurt now enabled him to encounter other aspects of reality: forgiveness, hope, and salvation (vv. 19-39). Accordingly, the tone of the composition changes radically to the positive in verse 19; the check word of verse 1, "affliction," is no longer the thesis; it has changed to prayer. It is only too true that he had persistently dwelt upon his sufferings and had consequently become despondent, but new dimensions of hope and of God break into his darkness; he recalled that the love of Yahweh entered the tragic scene. It came—everlasting, enduring, perenially new, bringing with it the faithfulness (truthfulness, fidelity) of Yahweh. Grasping in faith for God whose love, mercies, and fidelity encourage, the formerly depressed sufferer now identifies with Yahweh and joyfully confesses him to be his portion and his hope.

Such release from his plight generated within his heart an urge to testify, to witness that what had happened to him may become the experience of all if they would but follow the steps he has chosen. Accordingly, there was an expansion of moral sentiments in verses 22-39, instructing the hearers concerning the available saving grace (compare Pss. 32:8 ff.; 34:11 ff.).

The speaker extolled Yahweh, commending him as one who is good to those who wait for him, to those that seek him, to those that hope for his salvation. Even youth will be guided through the restive years when they need divine discipline the most. One notices the thesis of verses 25-27 in the word "good" which is repeated in the successive verses.

In verse 27 the admonition is given that it is good for a man to bear the yoke in his youth. The figure of the "yoke" suggests the reasonable service a person ought to perform in his relationship to his divine master (Matt. 11:29-30; negatively, Jer. 2:20; 5:5). It is well to bear this responsibility early in life, to endure the discipline which educates, to refrain from the bitter explosions of empty-headedness, even to endure in hopeful anticipation the yoke that holds you tight. It would appear that the speaker was addressing himself to the suffering Exilic community to be patient in its trials and hopeful of a blessed outcome.

This encouragement to endure is buttressed in the nature of God who will not forever cast off. If there is momentary grief, there will be compassion and abundance of love (vv. 31-33). His seeming harsh judgments were not willingly inflicted. They originated in his wisdom and compassion; so it may be inferred.

To build up his case, the poet drew attention to the character of God and listed some relevant, unethical principles Yahweh repudiates. Yahweh would not crush the imprisoned. He would not refuse to hear the right of man, and he would not subvert a man in his cause (vv. 31-36). It follows, then, that Yahweh was equitable. His ways are directed to the welfare of mankind. Why should man complain, therefore, about the recompense due his sins? The poet implied that the divine judgment was both equitable and wise. The recompense should be regarded as redemptive rather than punitive. (vv. 37-39).

The Individual Psalm of Lament, Part 2 (3:40-66)

The description of distress (vv. 40-54).—Were it not for the alphabetic arrangement, one would consider verses 40 and 41 to be part of the moralizing of the first psalm, inasmuch as this is an exhortation addressed to the company listening to the testimonial of the speaker and encouraging them to examine their lives and turn to Yahweh even though heretofore he had not forgiven them (v. 42). This refusal on the part of Yahweh to forgive is paralleled in Jeremiah, particularly in chapter 15, where after a moving penitential petition, Yahweh rejected the plea for forgiveness (15:1-4; compare 14:7-12,19-20). The reason Yahweh withheld his forgiveness was the insincerity and hypocrisy of the people's intent.

The public confession of sin (v. 42) which had been previously presented to Yahweh has been refused—so it would seem. The poet indicated some additional, disturbing occurrences that had further caused the divine alienation. Yahweh had clothed himself in anger, pursued, and slain the community; he had refused prayer with no repentance. He had permitted his people to be scoffed at by the nations and treated as refuse, particularly when the enemies witness the destruction he had visited upon his own people (vv. 45-47). In consequence, the poet's tears flowed copiously because of the destruction of the daughter of his people (v. 48).

His tears will not cease until Yahweh reverses the insufferable plight of his people, from which he selected a cause: the fate of the maidens of Jerusalem in which assault, rape, and enslavement by the soldiers of Babylon seem implied (vv. 49-51). Speaking in the name of the city, the poet lamented that the enemies had hunted him like a bird, casting him into the pit (the tomb) and hurling rocks upon him. The pit appears to have been a cistern in which water lay; the lamenter felt the water closing in over his head and that death was imminent (vv. 52-54; compare Ps. 69:1 ff.).

Prayer, oracle, and deliverance (vv. 55-66).—The climax of the lament is in verse 54, where the poet reached utter impotence and confessed: "I am lost." It is at that moment that God entered with his transforming power. The psalm now assumes the character of an individual psalm of thanksgiving with themes of divine deliverance and the testimony of the rescued. The speaker had called upon the name of Yahweh from the depths of the pit; and, what is more important, that prayer was answered (vv. 55 ff.; compare v. 8). The deliverance is announced in an oracle (a normal formula in the individual psalm of lament) in verse 56. Yahweh heard the plea, drew near, and comforted the suppliant with reassurance. This redemption appears to be effected by the summary judgment of Yahweh to be imposed upon the tormentors.

The composition passes from the deliverance to an imprecatory prayer. It is petitioned in verse 59 that those who have perpetrated such sufferings be recompensed because of their evil devices (vv. 59-60), their vicious slander perennially voiced, and their rude scoffing (vv. 61-64). The imprecation suggests that Yahweh give them dullness of mind, the divine curse, and ultimate judgment (v. 65 f.). Such moods are discoverable in the so-called imprecatory psalms within the Psalter (for example, 35, 58, 59, 69, and 109) and in Jeremiah (10:25; 17:18; 18:21-23; 22:12). This type of eye for an eye recompense is repudiated by our Lord in his words (Matt. 5:38 ff.) and in his works (Luke 23:34).

Chapter 4

The setting in life of this chapter appears to be Exilic (v. 22). The scene described in verse 17 is presented in reflection of the vain hopes the defenders of Jerusalem attached to the promised support from the Egyptians. The composition differs from chapters 1, 2, and 3 in that each verse has only two lines.

The distinguishing characteristic of this chapter is the intensity of the lament motif. This intensity is achieved by studied reference to the different participants among the Judeans who have experienced the horrors and rigors of the Babylonian assault. Starving nurslings, pampered rich, princes, hunger victims, compassionate mothers guiltily turned cannibalistic, sinful prophets and priests, and the Lord's anointed all are reviewed in their pathetic plight. Acknowledgment of sin as the cause of the disaster is voiced three times (vv. 6,13,22), four times if one includes verse 11. The focus proceeds from the situation of one group to another. The composition is a pure lament (vv. 1-20), with the final two verses introducing a related theme, a satirical imprecation upon sinful Edom (vv. 21-22). Unlike chapter 3, there is here no prayer, no hope expressed or faith affirmed, no moralization—nothing but frustration, suffering, and bewilderment. The lament is basically a unit and resembles those *pure* laments where the psalmist pours out the sorrows of his heart, having nothing to say, no prayer to utter, nothing but the over-whelming sorrow of his heart (compare Ps. 88).

The Horror in Jerusalem (4:1-16)

With the pathetic outcry "How!", an interjection of despair which begins chapters 1 and 2, the poet selected a fitting symbol to press home his point of the startling contrast between the past and the present. The symbol of gold ("pure gold" is fairly synonymous with "gold" in v. 1) with its glittering beauty and extreme preciousness was chosen to represent what Jerusalem once was. Now all that had been changed. The gold had become tarnished and deteriorated. Moreover, the stones of the sanctuary lie strewn about at every street corner, an unimaginable degradation and profanation! But while the Temple and its surrounding gold have suffered so, the precious sons of Zion, worth their weight in gold, have likewise endured the gross humiliation of the Babylonian attack. They who were once so treasured are now valueless, as depleted as a piece of common pottery, and they were sons of Zion, not metal! (vv. 1-2).

The scene shifts now to view the plight of the nursing mothers and their children in the surrounded city. The poet was attempting to emphasize the dire circumstances to which the population of Jerusalem had been subjected. In building his forceful expression the poet cites the mother love of a wild jackal who offers her breasts and suckles carefully her young. Then follows the shocking contrast. So harsh has been the siege of Jerusalem, so acute have been the pangs of hunger that nursing mothers have become insensible to moral standards and to the vital needs of their suckling children and have cruelly refused to feed both those at the breast and their little children, consigning them to certain starvation (vv. 3-4). Combined with the cannibalism in the city (2:20) and starvation (1:11; 2:11-12), the poet painted a picture of ethical disintegration under the duress of the siege (vv. 3-4).

The pampered rich are next placed under review. Those who once feasted on dainties and were brought up in purple now perish in the streets and lie on dung heaps (v. 5). Here for a moment the poet contemplated the immensity of the tragedy and transgression: Judah's sin far outstrips the infamous disaster of Sodom and Gomorrah. A nostalgic note enters in the expression: "the daughter of my people," a diminutive term sometimes rendered as "my poor people." The juxtaposition of this tenderness and the harshness everywhere else augments the contrast and the sorry plight of the suffering of the people (vv. 5-7).

The princes of Judah are now pictured, in their former dignity and their present indignity. The poet described the nobility in their earlier superb physical appearance: their complexions purer than snow (that is, without blemishes) and whiter than milk (that is, no swarthy complexions); their bodies more ruddy than coral and the beauty of their form like lapis lazuli. While the rendering of the Hebrew is somewhat uncertain, the general tenor of the words is clear: in face and form the princes and nobles were well-endowed, handsome, and well-proportioned. But now, plagued with malnutrition and denied water in which to bathe, their faces are blacker than soot. They are hardly recognizable in the streets with their thinness and dehydration. It would have been better to have been slain by the sword than to perish of hunger with all its attendant misery (vv. 7-9).

The poet returned to the plight of the infants and now described the shocking practice of cannibalism during the siege. Compassionate mothers were so depersonalized by hunger that they boiled and ate their own children rather than starve (v. 10). With such ultimate atrocities and indescribable horrors within the city, the writer unveiled the apocalyptic cause of the tragedy: it was Yahweh who in his wrath and anger had kindled a fire in Zion to consume it to its very foundations (v. 11). Such a calamity as had befallen Jerusalem was envisioned by no one. Kings and dwellers on earth would not have predicted such a terrible fate; it was unforeseen and unanticipated. No one could believe that Jerusalem would ever be taken (vv. 10-12).

The lament returns to the personnel within the city; the prophets and priests are now evaluated. Pinpointing the blame for the Judean disaster, the poet singled out the errors of the prophets and the iniquity of the priests. In the pursuit of their misguided policies they liquidated their opponents and shed the blood of the righteous. Whether indirectly or by persuasion of the civil authorities, foul murders were committed whose instigation was laid at the door of the religious personnel. When their plans blew up and destroyed the nation, they wandered aimlessly through the streets, stunned, groping blindly as they wandered. Their former devotees, so completely disillusioned by their tragic policies and predictions, regarded them now as unclean and untouchable. Like lepers to be shunned men ostracized them from their company crying, "Away! Away! Touch Not" (verse 15, compare Lev. 13:45). The once highly-respected clergy were expelled with disdain from the community and, like Cain of old, became fugitives and wanderers, a rootless and discredited caste. Even the nations to which the clerics emigrated deported them, refusing to allow them to live among them. Behind the scenes was Yahweh judging the corrupt clergy, scattering them, disregarding and dishonoring both priests and their colleagues, the elders (city magistrates) (vv. 13-16).

The Help That Did Not Come (4:17-20)

The poet penned the great expectations that the Judeans had anticipated from the Egyptians, the persistent hopes, the extended waiting for assistance, but, alas, it was all in vain. Egypt was impotent to save, as Jeremiah had so frequently warned (Jer. 2:18,36; 37:7 ff.).

Attention is now given to the harrassment of the last days of Judah when all in the open country were pursued by the swift Babylonian troops who chased their victims in the mountains and lay in wait in the wilderness for them. Under surveillance, harried by constant vigil, the Judeans felt unsafe even in the city streets. They sensed the end was ominously near, the days seemed numbered, and the end came (v. 18 is a moving climax). The king ("the breath of our nostrils, the Lord's anointed," v. 20) was captured by the Babylonians (Jer. 52:7), and the forlorn hope of dwelling safely as a nation under his leadership proved foolish (vv. 17-20).

The Punishment of Edom (4:21-22)

The poet cannot rid his thoughts of the treachery that Edom maliciously wrought at the fall of Jerusalem. For the moment the poet told Edom to enjoy the fleeting period of success, for soon Edom will have to drink of the cup of wrath from which Judah drank. Judah has paid for her iniquity; Edom will soon be called to account for her iniquity. The national sins of Edom will be uncovered and the punishment, so well deserved, will be meted out. It is an imprecatory wish involving the deceitful Edomites, once allies, now gloating, opportunistic enemies (vv. 21-22). (Compare the duplicity and treachery of Edom in Ps. 137:7-9; Obad. 5 ff.; Ezek. 25:12 ff.)

Epilogue

The last sound fades into silence; the curtain closes the stage; the drama is over. And yet the haunting lyrics ring within our minds, and the portrayed tragedy give cause for serious reflection. We cannot shake off the deep impression the characters have made upon us; they have challenged us to our very depths. We see a battered, war torn, lonely people, seemingly meaningless, exiled, and impoverished; and yet there is down deep within, a sorrow, a penitence that the woeful events produced, a longing for the better in life, a search after meaning, a movement toward God. They found God, and they were healed of their spiritual ills. They saw the plans and purposes of God; they identified with them. It was a slow process. It involved suffering, misunderstanding, and frustration, but on they went and became the people of God once again and earned praise: "Behold my servant, whom I uphold" (Isa. 42:1), and "I will give you as a light to the nations" (Isa. 49:6). Out of the darkness came light; out of the lamentations came joy. It was a godly sorrow that worked repentance.

Chapter 5

This chapter differs from the other four chapters in that it is not alphabetic. However, there are twenty-two verses of one line each, the number of letters in the Hebrew alphabet. The meter is not that of a *qinah* format $(3+2)$, the poetic type that appears in the other four chapters. The setting of the composition appears quite clearly to be that of the Exile (vv. 2,8,18,21), most likely several decades after the fall of Jerusalem in 587 BC. The form of the composition is that of an extended prayer with which the psalm opens (v. 1). There follows a long description of distress, which serves as the motivation for answering the petition (vv. 2-18). This lament may be subdivided in three parts: (1) the fate of those who remained in Judah/Jerusalem and their bitter personal experiences (vv. 2-6); (2) the harsh, incompetent government (vv. 8-16a); and (3) the affliction of devastated Mount Zion (vv. 17 ff.). A confession of sin and guilt concludes the first two parts of the lament: verse 7 at the end of verses 2-6 and verse 16b as a conclusion to verses 8-16a. A prayer climaxes the poem (vv. 19-22). It begins with an affirmation of the permanence of

Yahweh's kingdom (v. 19), then draws inferences and prayer petitions from that assertion (vv. 20-22).

The Prayer Proper (5:1)

Prayers are seldom encountered in the Book of Lamentations; there are only seven examples (1:9,11,20,22; 2:20-22; 3:19,35; 5:1). The petition here is couched in very general terms with no suggestion of what should be done in the circumstances. What concerned the writer exclusively were the disgrace and indescribable events that had unfortunately overtaken his people. Rather than succumb to pessimism, the writer appealed to God for restoration and renewal.

The Description of Distress, Part I: The Bitter Personal Experience of the Remnant in Judah (5:2-7)

The author sketched the insufferable privations accorded those that were left behind in Judah. They had been deprived of their homes and lands (v. 2). They had become orphaned and fatherless. Mothers with their husbands in exile were like widows (v. 3). The economic poverty of the Judeans was so severe that they must pay for the very basics of life: water to drink and wood for cooking or fuel (v. 4). Slave labor was oppressive as unreasonable demands were imposed (v. 5). Some attempting to escape the exacting economy in Judah migrated to Egypt and Assyria to ward off starvation (v. 6). All these calamities were attributed to the sins of their deceased fathers. Since they had not paid the penalty it had fallen upon their descendants. The notion of corporate guilt was firmly entrenched in Israelite thought. It was, indeed, an inheritance from their ancient cultural tradition. While it has a small amount of truth in it, it was challenged and modified in the religious teachings of the prophets (Jer. 31:29; Ezek. 18; compare Deut. 24:16; 2 Kings 14:6; 2 Chron. 25:4). The confession of their predecessors' sins was candidly and frankly united with an acknowledgement of their own sins (v. 16*b*).

Part 2: The Harsh, Incompetent Government (5:8-16)

The poet deplored the oppressive rule of the Babylonian provincial functionaries, whose sole interest was in maintaining the policies dictated by their overlords in Babylon. Their administration was directed toward the interests of the victorious conquerors, which were slavishly pursued despite the frustrations such a rule must have occasioned their subjects. In unvarnished terms the poet described these rulers as slaves, and the proverb is quite appropriate that "the earth trembles" when a slave has become a king (Prov. 30:21). One can only imagine how the boorishness, the disdain, and the ineptitude of the foreign provincial magistrates must have irritated the Judeans and thwarted any speedy hopes of recovery. It was a system imposed upon the vanquished from which there was no appeal or escape.

Such abuse of power made itself felt in the scarcity of food. There was danger in working the fields without the protection of an informed and stable government (v. 9). Famine resulted with pathological results of fever (v. 10). Women were ravished with impunity within the Judean cities (v. 11). Princes were hung by their hands, and elders were dishonored. The youth were pressed into slave labor and made to grind at the mill or haul loads of wood (v. 13). Scenes of yesterday, including the city gates—once the favored resort of the old men—were deserted. The young men, once delighting in song and and dance, now had lost heart for such and preferred the lament. Universal despair pervaded the life of every one in the subjugated kingdom of Judah. The government, the food situation, the national health, the unavenged crimes, the barbaric executions, the curtailed activities, and the encompassing depression—all of this may be summed up in the words: "The crown has fallen from our head" (v. 16). Most significant was the confession of national sin immediately attached to the recital of the hardships. There was a reason behind the strange set of events: it was Yahweh visiting them because of their sin (v. 16b).

The Affliction of Mount Zion (5:17-18)

The psychosomatic influence felt by the Judeans over the desolation of Mount Zion, whose destruction was complete since "jackals prowl over it," had caused a sickness of heart (mind) and an eye trouble. The thought of it was sickening; when they attempted to visualize the future, they were unable.

The Prayer (5:19-22)

The poet made a strong case for his prayer by declaring directly to Yahweh that his kingdom is forever (v. 19). If Yahweh is King of all time, he is also then King of every particular historical situation. Two matters may immediately be deduced from this affirmation.

First, it is paradoxical that the Judeans should be forgotten and forsaken by Yahweh, as their present circumstances strongly suggest, since Yahweh is the Lord of all and since he is the God of the Judeans. Something is wrong somewhere. Second, it certainly could not be that Yahweh has utterly rejected us. It might possibly be that Yahweh is still angry with us (v. 22). And he has a right to be disturbed with us, but we are disturbed with ourselves and have sincerely confessed our sins. Then follows the prayer (in its use in the synagogue v. 21 is placed after v. 22) to be restored (turned) to Yahweh that they may be restored (to themselves) and to the good years of yesterday (compare Jer. 31:18 ff.).